budgetbooks

ACOUSTIC SONGS

ISBN 978-1-4768-8965-8

DISTRIBUTED BY

HAL•LEONARD®

Visit Hal Leonard Online at
www.halleonard.com

CONTENTS

AGAINST THE WIND

Words and Music by
BOB SEGER

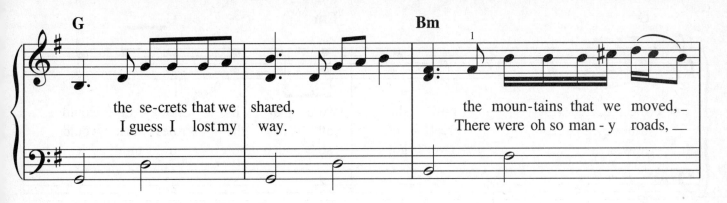

the se-crets that we shared,
I guess I lost my way.

the moun-tains that we moved, _
There were oh so man - y roads, _

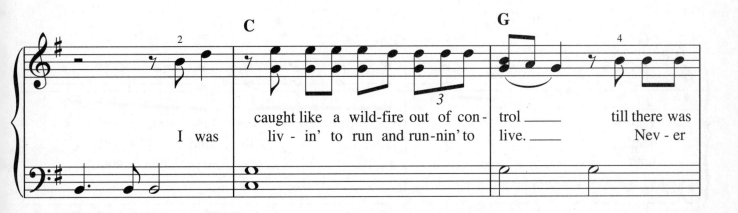

I was
caught like a wild-fire out of con-trol _____
liv - in' to run and run-nin' to live. _____

till there was
Nev - er

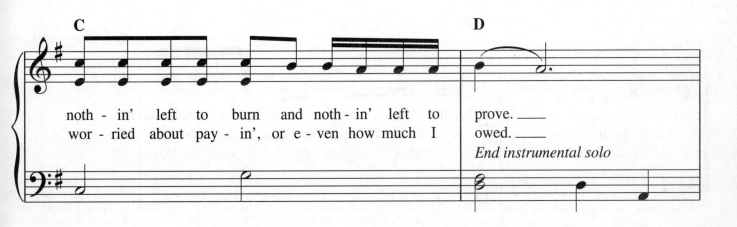

noth - in' left to burn and noth - in' left to prove. _____
wor - ried about pay - in', or e - ven how much I owed. _____

End instrumental solo

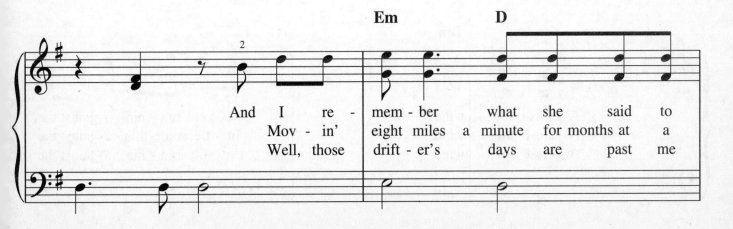

And I re - mem - ber what she said to
Mov - in' eight miles a minute for months at a
Well, those drift - er's days are past me

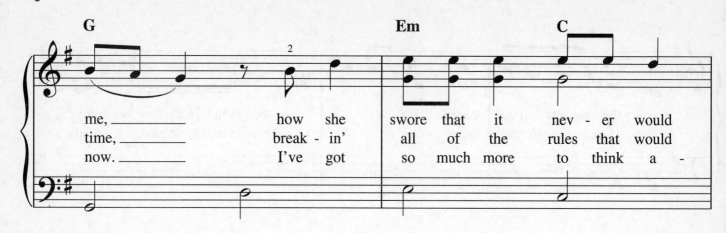

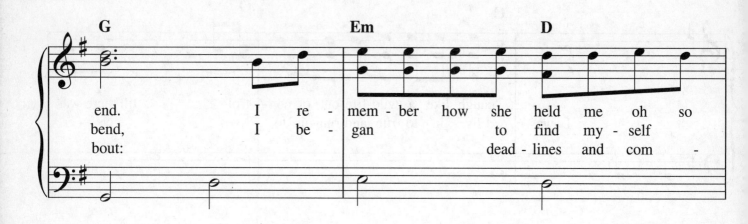

BARELY BREATHING

Words and Music by
DUNCAN SHEIK

star. The black-holes that sur-round you are heav-i-er by far. I be-lieved_ in your con-

fu - sion, so com-plete - ly torn._ It must have been_ that
ask - ing what's it all___ a - bout?_ It used to be___ so

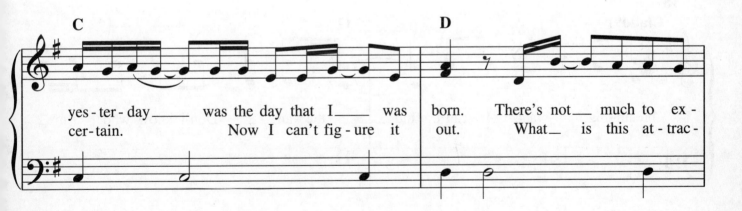

yes - ter - day___ was the day that I___ was born. There's not_ much to ex-
cer - tain. Now I can't fig-ure it out. What_ is this at-trac-

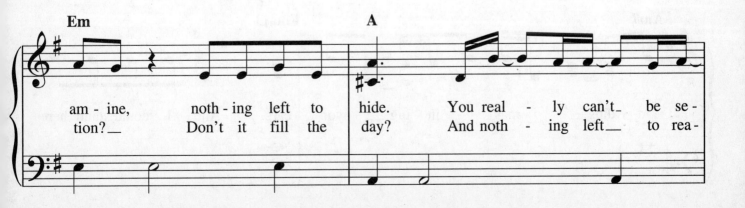

am - ine, noth - ing left to hide. You real - ly can't_ be se-
tion?_ Don't it fill the day? And noth - ing left_ to rea-

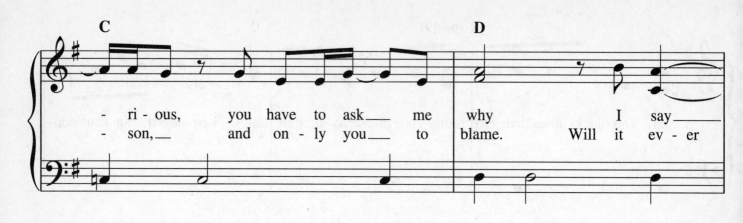

-ri-ous, you have to ask____ me why I say____
-son,____ and on-ly you____ to blame. Will it ev-er

____ good-bye.____
change?____ 'Cause I am bare-ly

breath-ing, and I can't find____ the air.____ Don't know who I'm____

kid-ding,____ i-mag-in-ing____ you care. And I could stand here

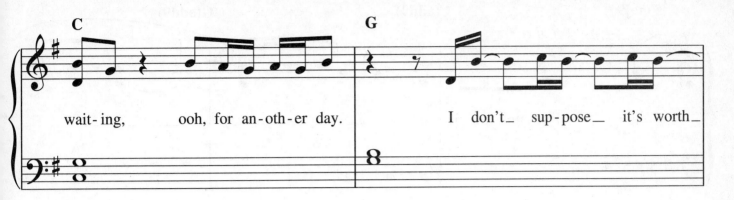

waiting, ooh, for an-oth-er day. I don't sup-pose it's worth

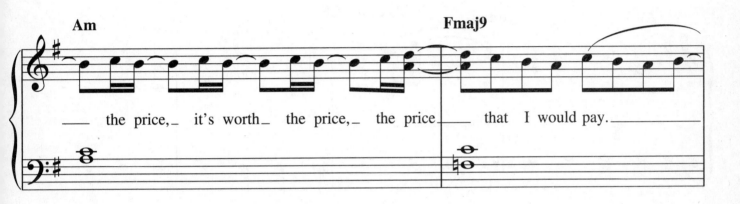

the price, it's worth the price, the price that I would pay.

And ev-'ry-one keeps

But I'm think-ing it o - ver an-y-way.

Fmaj9 ... **C(add9)** ... **G(add9)**

I'm think-ing it o - ver__ an - y - way.__

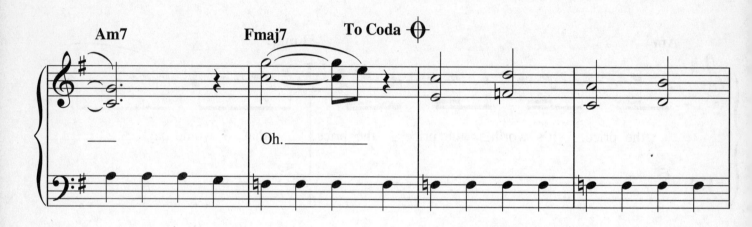

Am7 ... **Fmaj7** ... **To Coda**

Oh.__

D ... **Am**

I come to find__ I may__ nev-er know.__

Cmaj9 ... **Gm9** ... **D**

A chang - ing mind, is it friend__ or foe?__ I rise__ a-bove,

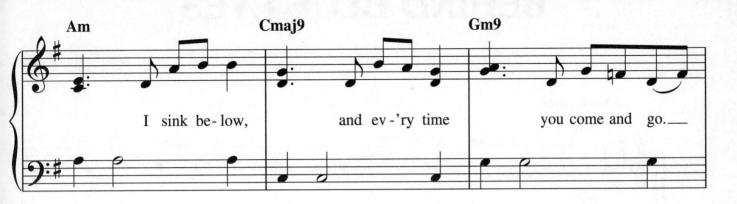

I sink be-low, and ev-'ry time you come and go.___

Please don't come and go.___

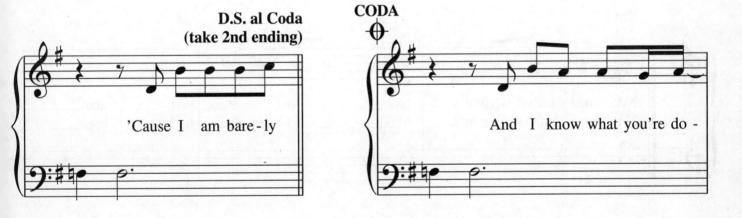

D.S. al Coda
(take 2nd ending)

'Cause I am bare-ly

CODA

And I know what you're do -

- ing.

I see it all___ too clear.

BEHIND BLUE EYES

Words and Music by
PETE TOWNSHEND

No one knows what it's like to be the bad man,
No one knows what it's like to feel these feel - ings

to be the sad man be -
like I do, and

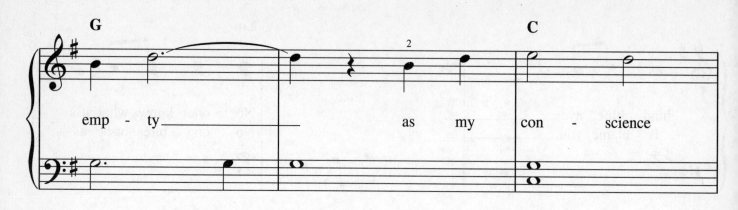

empty_____ as my con - science

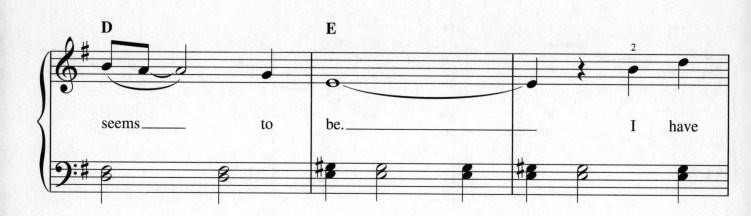

seems_____ to be._____ I have

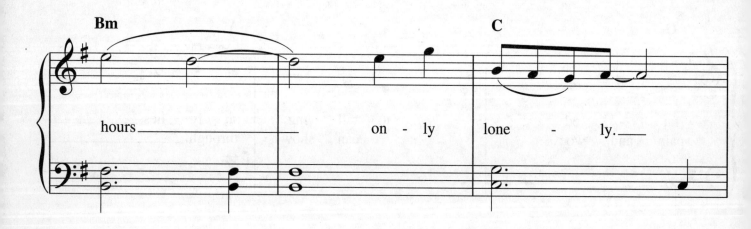

hours_____ on - ly lone - ly.___

My love is ven - geance that's nev - er

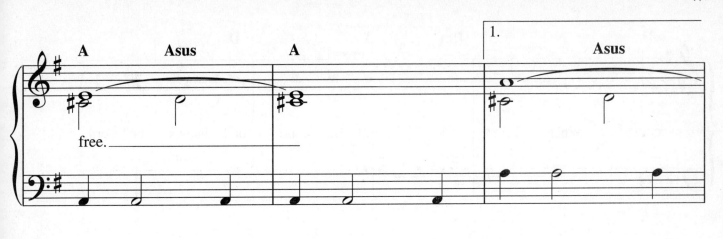

free.

When my fist

clench - es, crack it o - pen be - fore I use it and lose __ my

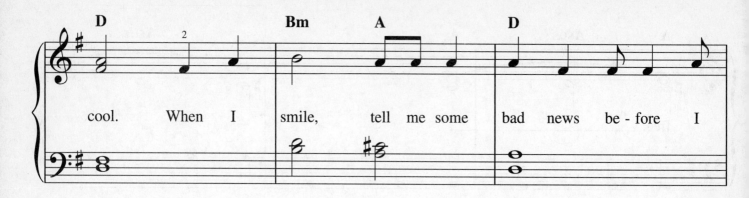

cool. When I smile, tell me some bad news be-fore I

laugh and act like a fool.

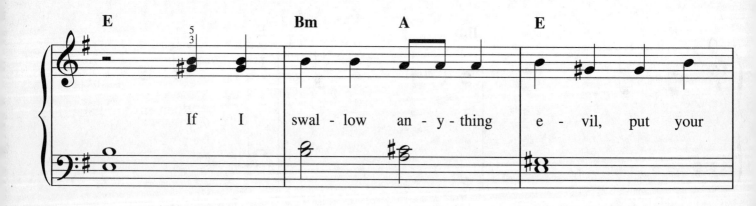

If I swal-low an-y-thing e-vil, put your

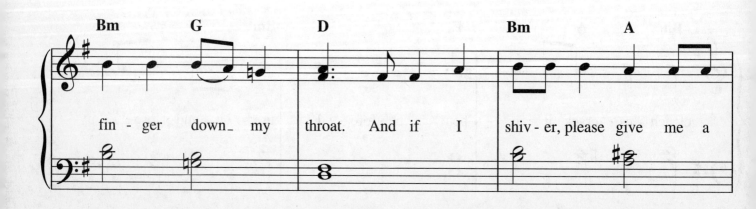

fin-ger down_ my throat. And if I shiv-er, please give me a

blan - ket. Keep me warm; let me wear your coat._____

_____ No one knows what it's like_____ to be the

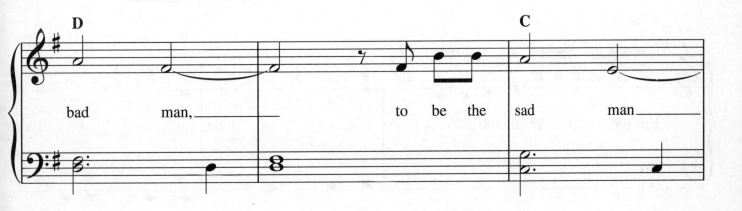

bad man,_____ to be the sad man_____

_____ be - hind blue eyes._____

BLACK HORSE AND THE CHERRY TREE

Words and Music by
KATIE TUNSTALL

Moderately, with a beat

Woo, hoo,___ woo, hoo, woo, hoo,___ woo,

hoo. Well, my heart knows me bet-ter than I know my-self so

I'm gon-na let it do all the talk-in'. Woo, hoo,___ woo, hoo. I

came a-cross a place in the mid-dle of no - where with a big black horse and a cher-ry tree. Woo,

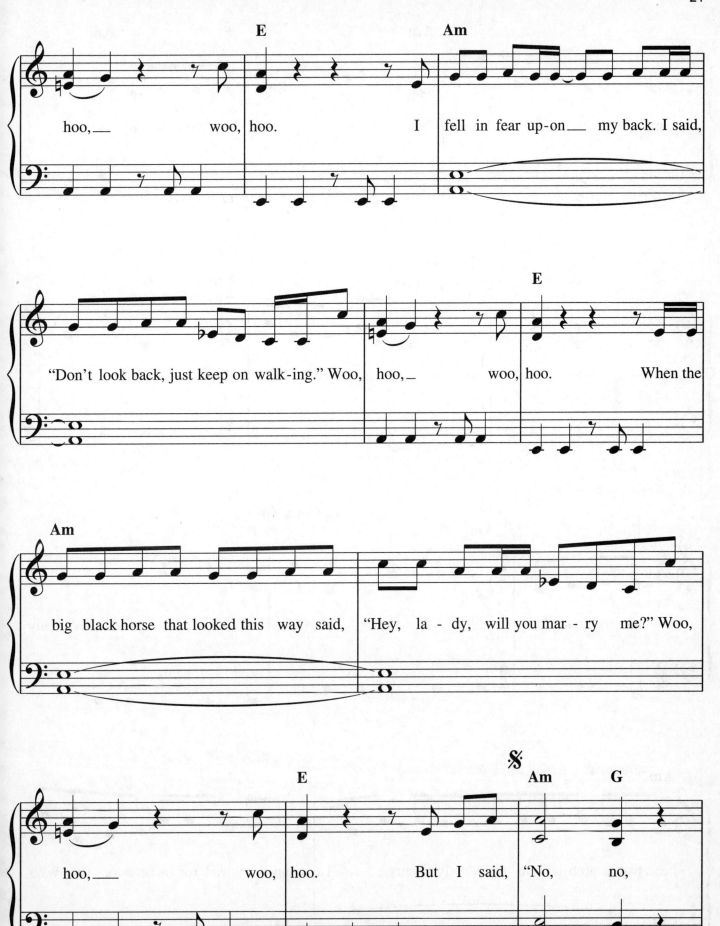

no, no, no, no." I said, "No, no, you're not the one for me.

No, no, no, no, no, no." I said, "No, no, you're

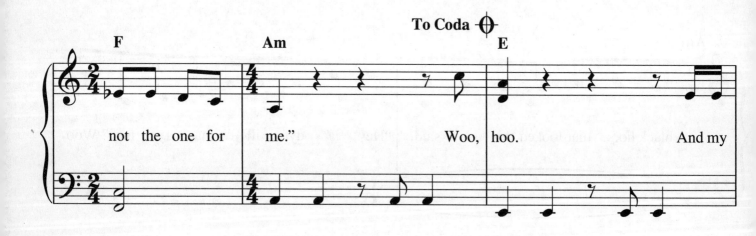

To Coda ⊕

not the one for me." Woo, hoo. And my

heart had a prob-lem in the ear - ly hours, so I stopped it dead for a beat or two. Woo,

hoo, _____ woo, hoo. But I

Am

cut some cord and I should-n't have done _ that, and it won't for-give _ me af-ter all these years. Woo,

E   **Am**

hoo, _ woo, hoo. So I sent her to a place in the mid-dle of no - where with a

E

big black horse and a cher-ry tree. Woo, hoo, _____ woo, hoo. Now it

Am

won't come back 'cause it's, oh, so hap-py, and now___ I got a hole for the world to see. Woo,

E **D.S. al Coda**

hoo,___ woo, hoo. And it said,

CODA

hoo.___ Woo,

E

hoo. Woo, hoo.

Am

I said, "No, no, no, no,

no, no, no, no, no,___ you're not the one for me.___

No, no, no, no, no, no, no, no, no,_____ you're

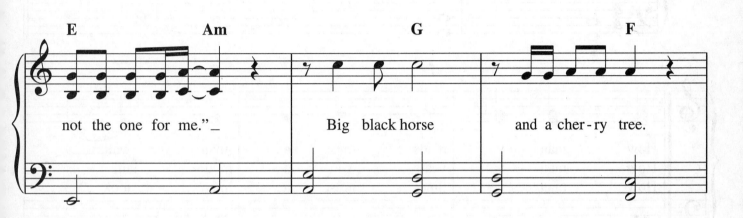

not the one for me."_ Big black horse and a cher-ry tree.

I can't quite get there 'cause my heart's for-sak-en me, yeah, yeah, yeah. Big black horse_____

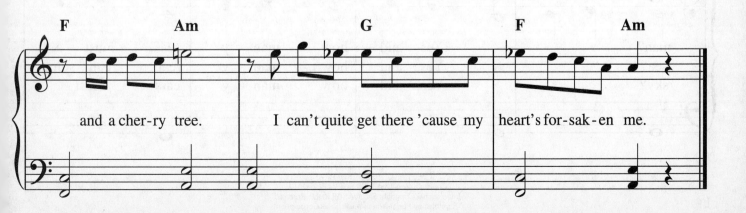

and a cher-ry tree. I can't quite get there 'cause my heart's for-sak-en me.

BLOWIN' IN THE WIND

Words and Music by
BOB DYLAN

27

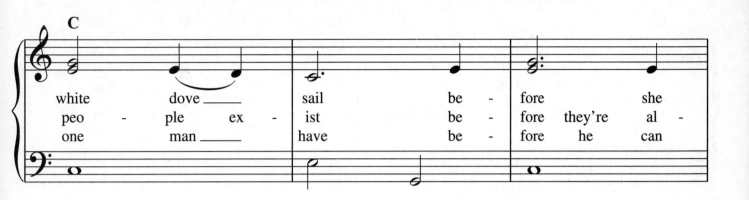

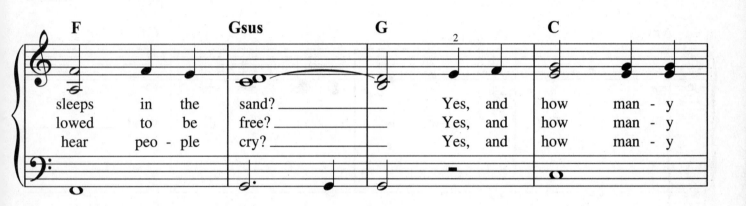

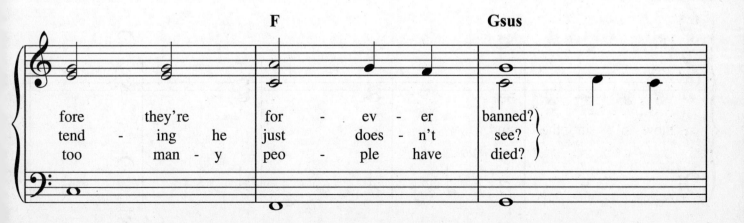

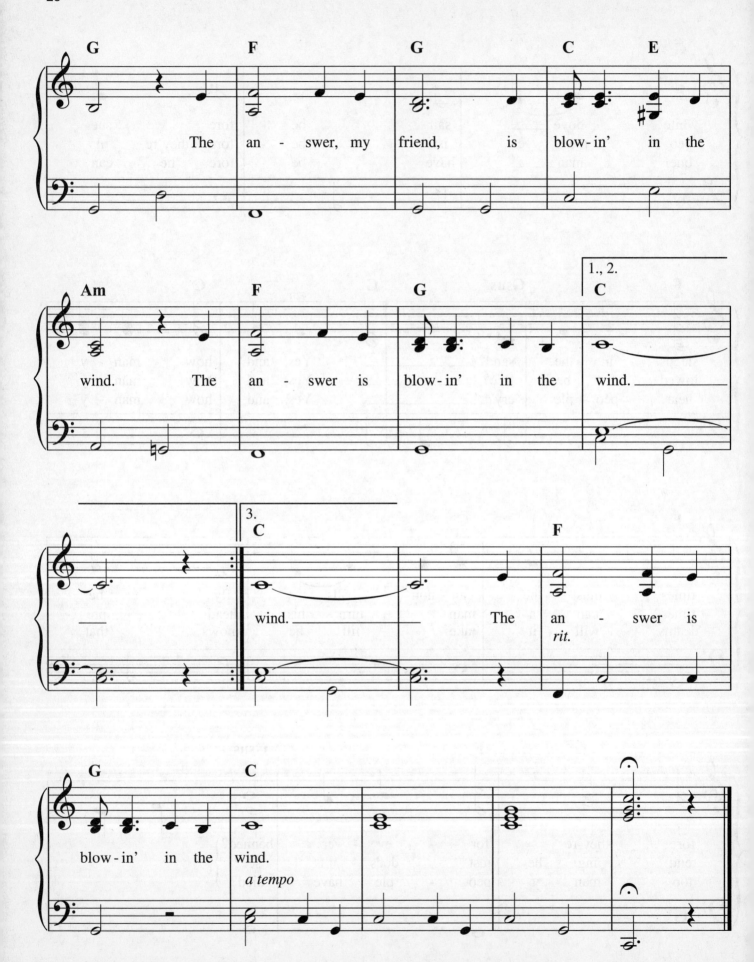

CAN'T FIND MY WAY HOME

Words and Music by
STEVE WINWOOD

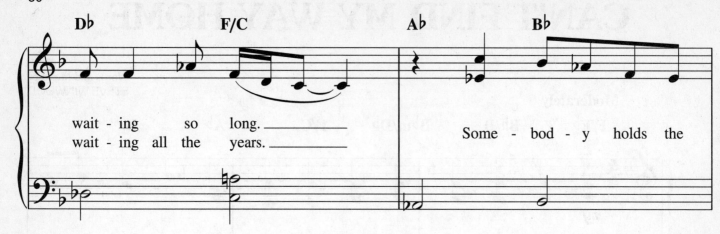

waiting so long. _____
wait - ing all the years. _____

Some - bod - y holds the

key. _____ Well, I'm near the end; __ I just ain't got __ the

time, be-cause I'm wast-ed and __ I can't find my way home. __

BOULEVARD OF BROKEN DREAMS

Words by BILLIE JOE
Music by GREEN DAY

I walk this emp-ty street on the bou-le-vard __ of bro-ken

CAT'S IN THE CRADLE

Words and Music by HARRY CHAPIN
and SANDY CHAPIN

My child ar-rived ____ just the oth-er day. ____ He came to the world in the

son turned ten ____ just the oth-er day. ____ He said, "Thanks for the ball, Dad. Come

came from col-lege just the oth-er day, ____ so much like a man I just

don't know when, but we'll get to - geth - er then. _____ You

know we'll have a good time then."

My
Well, he

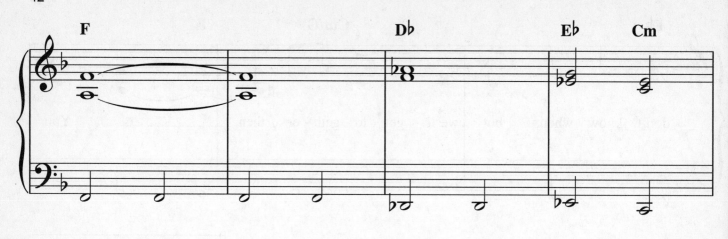

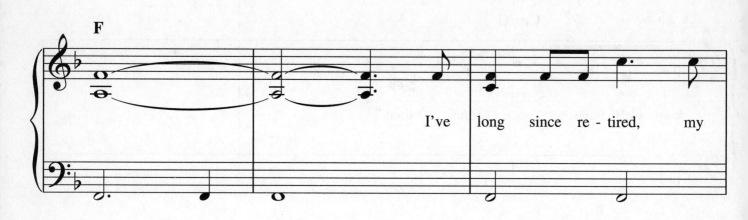

I've long since re-tired, my

son's moved a-way. I called him up just the oth-er day.

I said, "I'd like to see _____ you if

you don't mind." He said, "I'd love to, Dad, if I can

find the time. You see, my new job's a has-sle and the

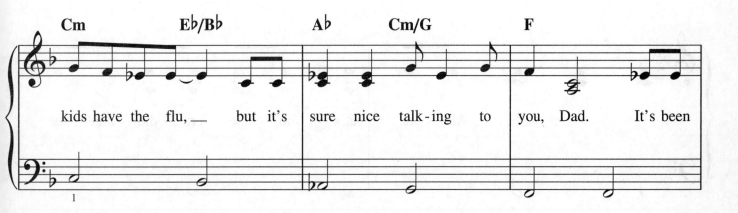

kids have the flu, but it's sure nice talk-ing to you, Dad. It's been

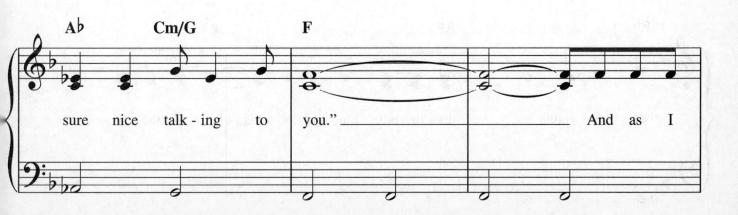

sure nice talk-ing to you." And as I

Eb **Eb/D** **Cm** **Eb/Bb** **Ab** **Cm/G**

hung up   the phone, it oc - cured   to   me, __   he'd   grown up   just   like

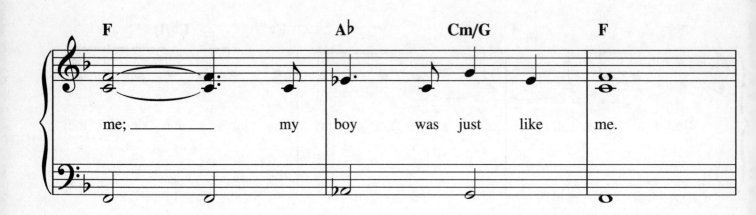

F **Ab** **Cm/G** **F**

me; _____   my   boy   was   just   like   me.

And   the   cat's   in   the   cra - dle   and   the

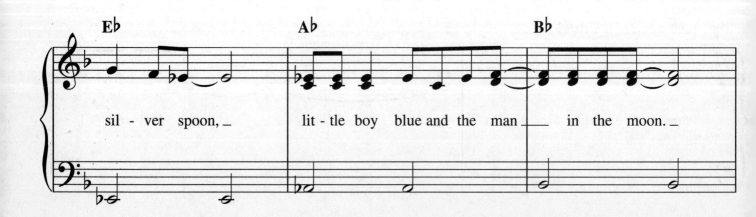

Eb **Ab** **Bb**

sil - ver spoon, _   lit - tle boy blue and the man __   in   the   moon. _

F

"When you com - ing home, son?" "I don't know when, but

E♭

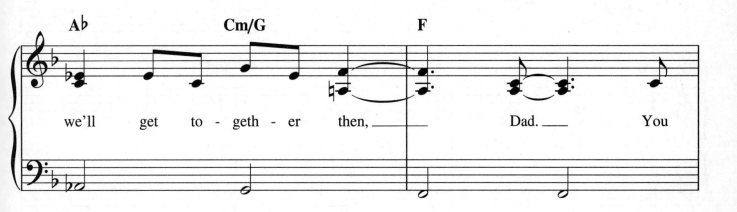

A♭　　**Cm/G**　　**F**

we'll get to - geth - er then,_____ Dad.___ You

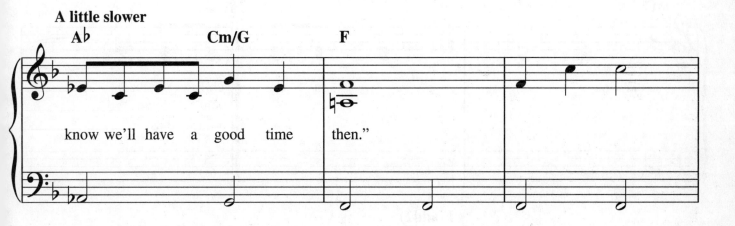

A little slower

A♭　　**Cm/G**　　**F**

know we'll have a good time then."

B♭/F　　**Fsus2**　　**Cm**　　**F**

CATCH THE WIND

Words and Music by
DONOVAN LEITCH

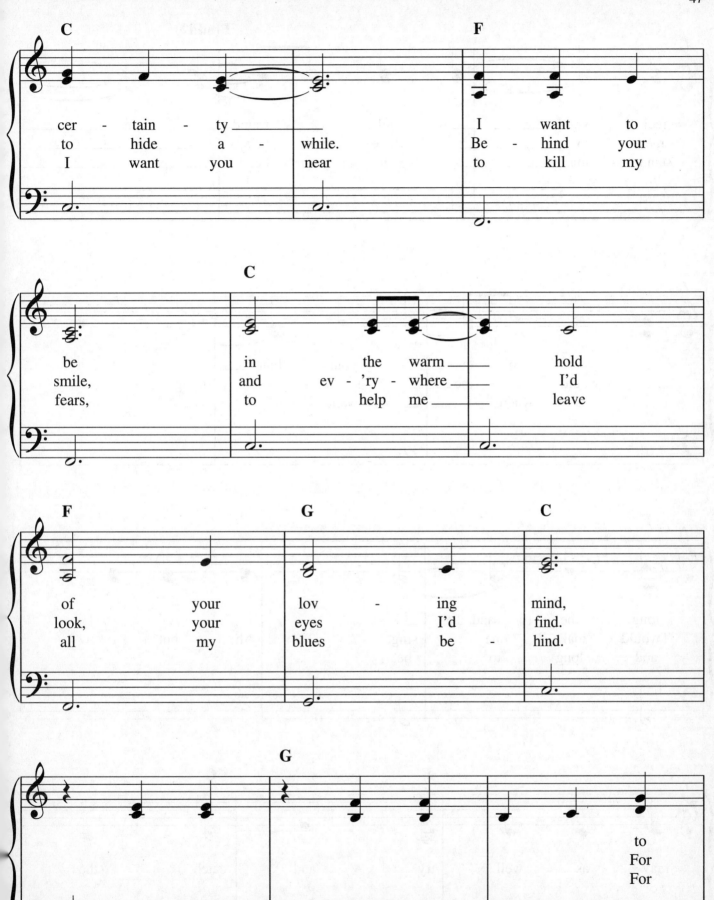

When

CODA

Instrumental

Instrumental ends   Ah,   but   I   may   as   well   try   and

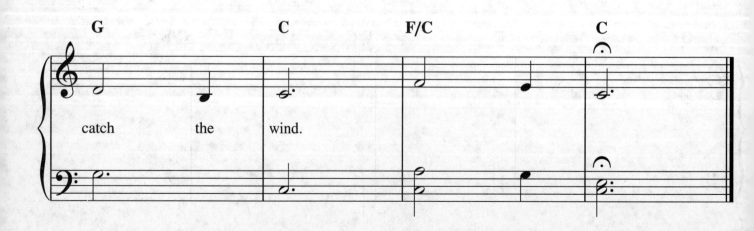

catch   the   wind.

COME MONDAY

Words and Music by
JIMMY BUFFET

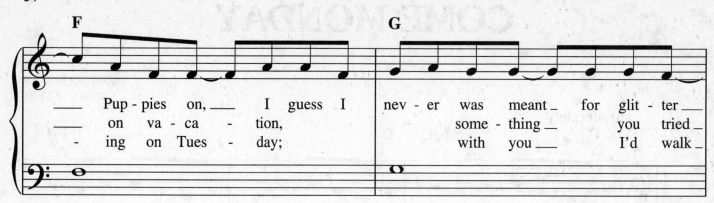

Pup - pies on, ___ I guess I
___ on va - ca - tion,
- ing on Tues - day;

nev - er was meant ___ for glit - ter ___
some - thing ___ you tried
with you ___ I'd walk ___

___ rock and roll. ___
___ to ex - plain. ___
___ an - y - where. ___

And hon - ey,
And dar - ling,
Cal - i - for - nia has

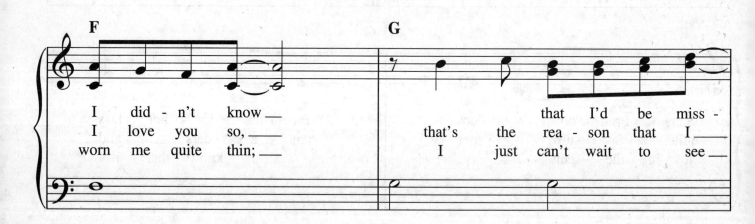

I did - n't know ___
I love you so, ___
worn me quite thin; ___

that I'd be miss -
that's the rea - son that I ___
I just can't wait to see

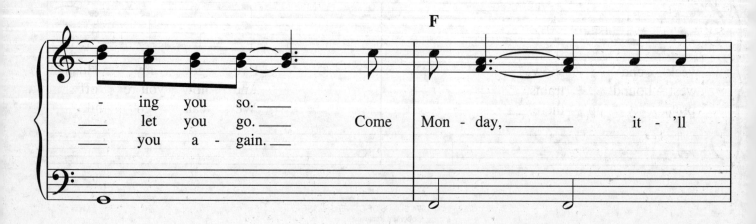

- ing you so. ___
___ let you go. ___
___ you a - gain. ___

Come Mon - day, ___ it - 'll

CHANGE THE WORLD

Words and Music by WAYNE KIRKPATRICK,
GORDON KENNEDY and TOMMY SIMS

CHASING CARS

Words and Music by GARY LIGHTBODY,
TOM SIMPSON, PAUL WILSON,
JONATHAN QUINN and NATHAN CONNOLLY

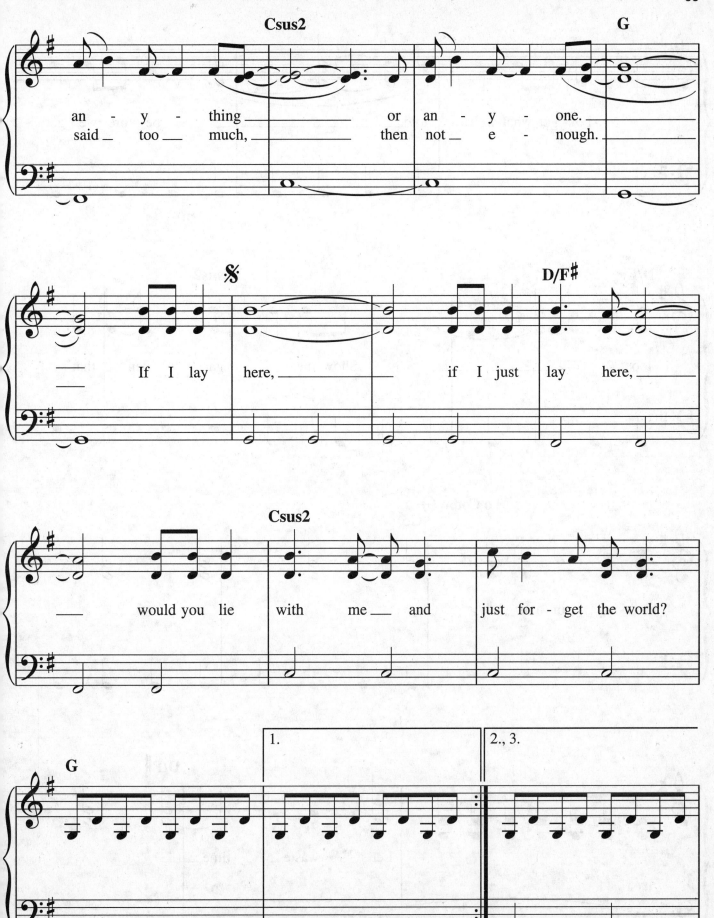

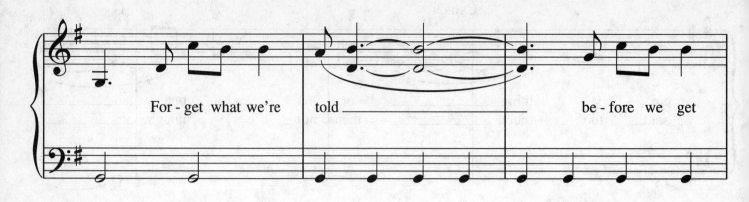

For - get what we're told _____ be - fore we get

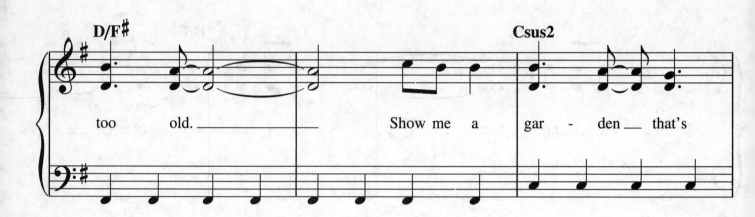

D/F#

Csus2

too old. _____ Show me a gar - den ___ that's

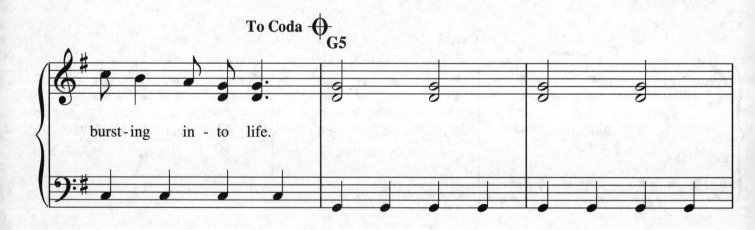

To Coda ⊕
G5

burst - ing in - to life.

D/F#

Let's waste ___ time ___

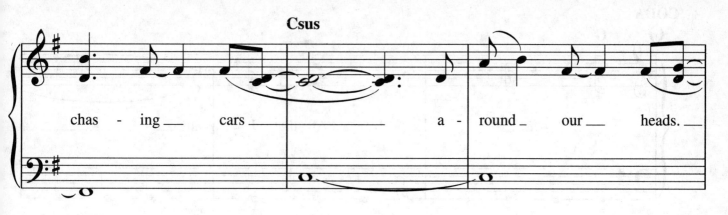

chas - ing___ cars_____ a - round___ our___ heads.___

___ I

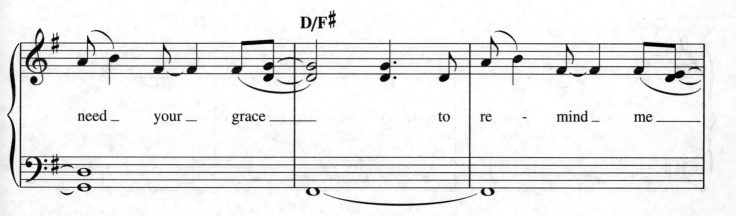

need___ your___ grace_____ to re - mind___ me___

_____ to find___ my___ own.___ If I lay

CODA

G

All that I am, _____

_____ all that I

D/F#

ev - er was _____ is here in your

Csus2

per - fect ___ eyes, they're all I can see.

G

I don't know where, _____ con-fused a-bout

how, as well._____ Just know that these things will nev - er change _

__ for us at all. If I lay here, _____

__ if I just lay here, _____ would you lie with me _ and

just for - get the world?

DANCE WITH ME

Words and Music by
JOHN and JOHANNA HALL

Upbeat Pop feel

(1., 3.) Dance with __ me, ___ I want __ to be your part - ner.
(2.) Fan - ta - sy ____ could nev - er be so kill - ing;

Can't you __ see, ___ the mu - sic is just start - ing?
I feel __ free, ___ I hope __ that you are will - ing.

Night is call - ing and I am fall - ing;
Pick the beat __ up and kick your feet _____ up;

dance with __ me. ____
dance with __ me. ____

To Coda

1.

the mu - sic is just start - ing? Night is call - ing and

I am fall - ing; dance with me.

DAUGHTER

Words and Music by STONE GOSSARD,
JEFFREY AMENT, EDDIE VEDDER,
MICHAEL McCREADY and DAVID ABBRUZZESE

ten - tion. _____ But   moth - er reads a - loud; child__

_____ tries to un - der - stand__ it, ____   tries to make__ her

proud.   The shades __ go   down, it's   in ___ her   head. __

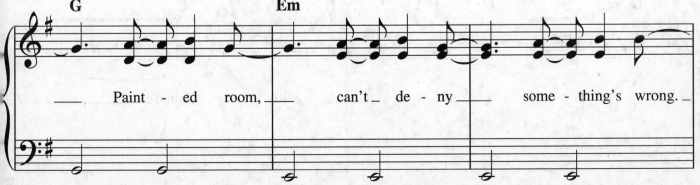

__ Paint - ed   room, ___   can't __ de - ny ___   some - thing's wrong. __

Play 3 times

Don't call ___ me ___ daugh-ter, ___ not fit ___ to.

The pic - ture kept ___ will re - mind ___

me. Don't call ___ me ___ daugh-ter, ___ not fit ___ to.

D.S. al Coda

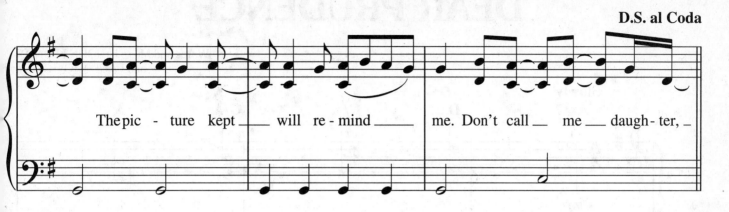

The pic - ture kept ___ will re - mind ___ me. Don't call ___ me ___ daugh - ter, ___

CODA

Play 3 times

Em

The shades go ___ down. ___ The shades ___ go ___

Repeat and Fade **Optional Ending**

G   **G**   **Em**

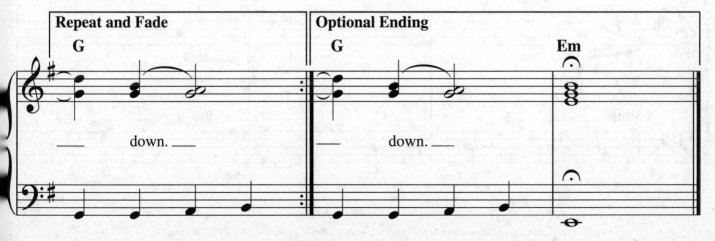

— down. ___ — down. ___

DEAR PRUDENCE

Words and Music by JOHN LENNON
and PAUL McCARTNEY

sun is up, ___ the sky is blue, _ it's beau - ti - ful _____ and

so are you. _____ Dear ___ Pru - dence, _ won't you come out to

play? _____

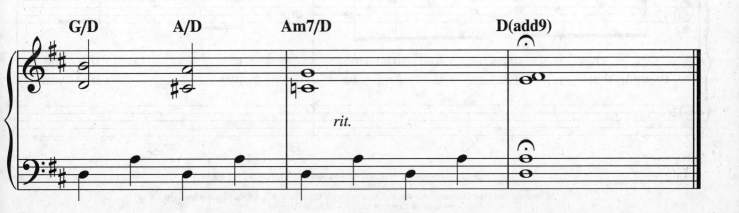

rit.

DO YOU BELIEVE IN MAGIC

Words and Music by
JOHN SEBASTIAN

Do you be-lieve in mag - ic ___ in a
- ic? ___ Just close

young girl's heart? ___ How the mu - sic can free ___ her when-
those big eyes, ___ and think all the won - der - ful

ev - er it starts? ___ And it's mag - ic ___ if the
thoughts that a - rise. ___ And ba - by, ___ if you

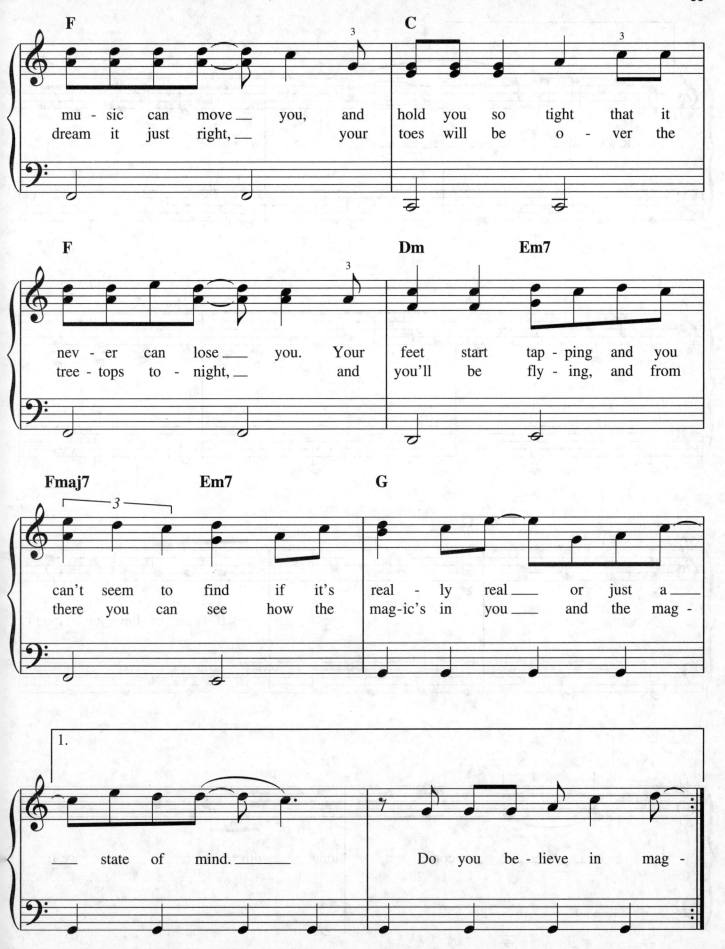

- ic's in ___ me. ___

If you be-lieve in mag-

- ic, _____ come a - long with me; ___ we'll

mag - ic's in the mu - sic and the mu - sic's in ___ me. ___

Be - lieve in the mag - ic of a

young girl's soul. ___ Be - lieve in the mag - ic of ___

DRIFT AWAY

Words and Music by
MENTOR WILLIAMS

Moderately fast

1. Day af - ter day I'm more con -
2.,3. *(See additional lyrics)*

fused;

I look for the

light in the pour - ing__ rain.__

CODA

strong. Give me the beat,_ boys, to soothe my soul; I

wan - na get lost in your rock and roll_____ and drift a - way._____

Additional Lyrics

2. Beginning to think that I'm wastin' time;
   Don't understand the things that I do.
   'Cause the world outside looks so unkind.
   Now I'm countin' on you to carry me through.
   Chorus

3. And thanks for the joy that you've given me;
   I want you to know I believe in your song,
   And rhythm and rhyme and harmony.
   You help me along, makin' me strong.
   Chorus

EVERYBODY'S TALKIN'

(Echoes)
from MIDNIGHT COWBOY

Words and Music by
FRED NEIL

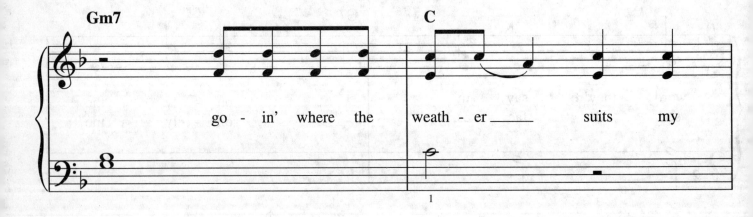

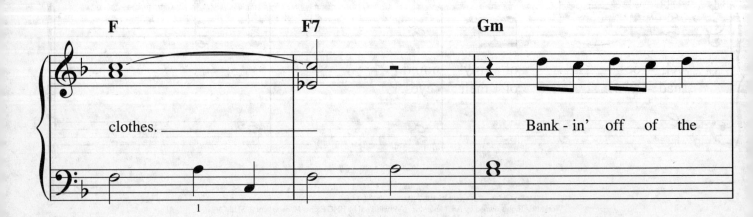

GIVE A LITTLE BIT

Words and Music by RICK DAVIES
and ROGER HODGSON

I'll give a lit-tle bit___ of my love to you. / life for you.

To Coda

There's so much___ that we need to share,___ so
Now's the time___ that we need to share,___ so

send a smile___ and show you care.___

I'll give a lit-tle bit,_____ I'll give a lit-tle bit___ of my

life for you. So give a lit-tle bit,_____

oh, give a lit-tle bit___ of your time to me.

See the man___ with the lone - ly eyes?___ Oh,

take his hand;_ you'll be sur - prised._

CODA

F   B♭   F

find your-self;___ we're on our way___ back

G   C/G   G   C/G   G   C/G

home.   Oh, go-in' home.

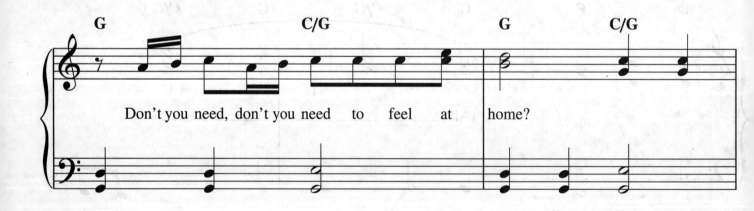

G   C/G   G   C/G

Don't you need, don't you need to feel at home?

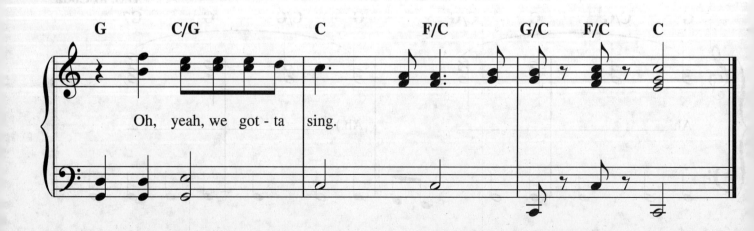

G   C/G   C   F/C   G/C F/C   C

Oh, yeah, we got-ta sing.

HALLELUJAH

Words and Music by
LEONARD COHEN

Additional Lyrics

2. Your faith was strong, but you needed proof.
   You saw her bathing on the roof.
   Her beauty and the moonlight overthrew you.
   She tied you to a kitchen chair.
   She broke your throne; she cut your hair.
   And from your lips she drew the Hallelujah.
   Chorus

3. Maybe I have been here before.
   I know this room; I've walked this floor.
   I used to live alone before I knew you.
   I've seen your flag on the marble arch.
   Love is not a victory march.
   It's a cold and it's a broken Hallelujah.
   Chorus

4. There was a time you let me know
   What's real and going on below.
   But now you never show it to me, do you?
   And remember when I moved in you,
   The holy dark was movin' too,
   And every breath we drew was Hallelujah.
   Chorus

5. Maybe there's a God above,
   And all I ever learned from love
   Was how to shoot at someone who outdrew you.
   And it's not a cry you can hear at night.
   It's not somebody who's seen the light.
   It's a cold and it's a broken Hallelujah.
   Chorus

HELPLESSLY HOPING

Words and Music by
STEPHEN STILLS

They are one ____ per - son, they are two___

a - lone, ____ they are three___ to - geth-

- er, they are for _____ each oth - er.

HEY THERE DELILAH

Words and Music by
TOM HIGGENSON

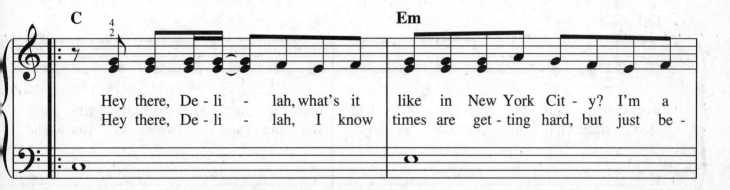

Hey there, De - li - lah, what's it like in New York Cit - y? I'm a
Hey there, De - li - lah, I know times are get - ting hard, but just be -

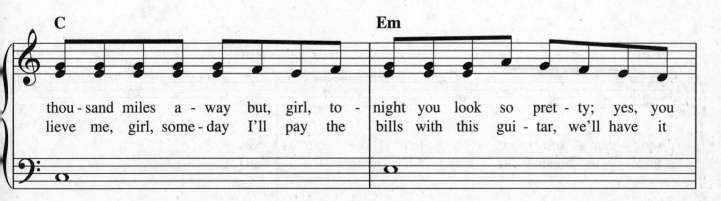

thou - sand miles a - way but, girl, to - night you look so pret - ty; yes, you
lieve me, girl, some - day I'll pay the bills with this gui - tar, we'll have it

do. / good.

Am — Times Square can't shine as bright as / We'll have the life we knew we

you. _____ I swear it's true. / would. _____ My word is good.

Hey there, De - li - lah, don't you / Hey there, De - li - lah, I've got

wor - ry a - bout the dis - tance. I'm right / too _ much left to say. If ev - 'ry

there. If you get lone - ly, give this / sim - ple song I wrote to you would

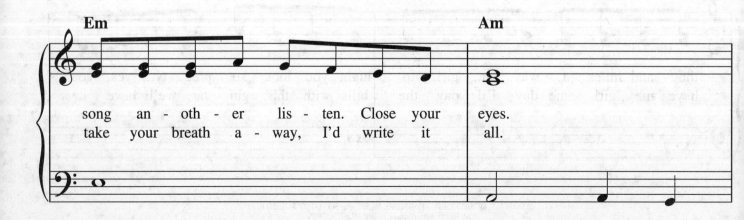

song an - oth - er lis - ten. Close your / take your breath a - way, I'd write it

eyes. / all.

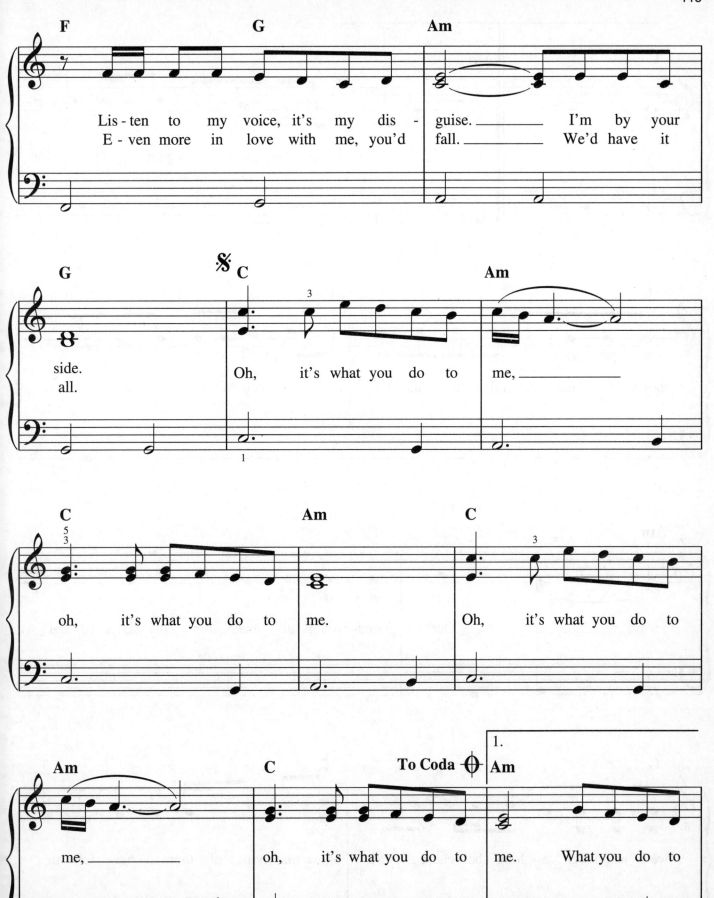

Lis-ten to my voice, it's my dis- guise. _____ I'm by your
E - ven more in love with me, you'd fall. _____ We'd have it

side.
all.

Oh, it's what you do to me, _____

oh, it's what you do to me. Oh, it's what you do to

me, _____ oh, it's what you do to me. What you do to

C me.

2. **Am** me. _____ A thou-sand miles seems pret-ty far ___ but

G they've got planes, and trains and cars. I'd

C walk to you if I had no oth - er

Am way. _____ Our

F friends would all make fun of us, ___ and

G we'll just laugh a - long be - cause_ we

C know that none of them_ have felt this

way._____ De - li - lah, I can prom - ise you __ that

by the time we get through __ the world will nev - er, ev - er be the

same,_____ and you're to blame._____

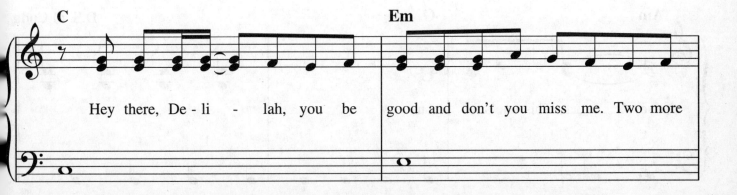

Hey there, De - li - lah, you be good and don't you miss me. Two more

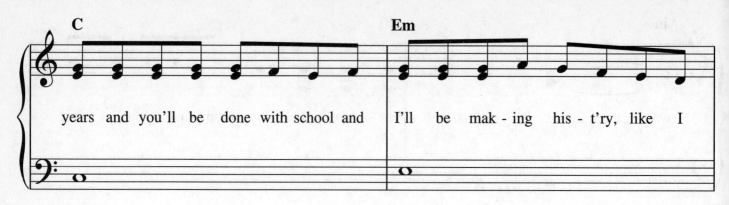

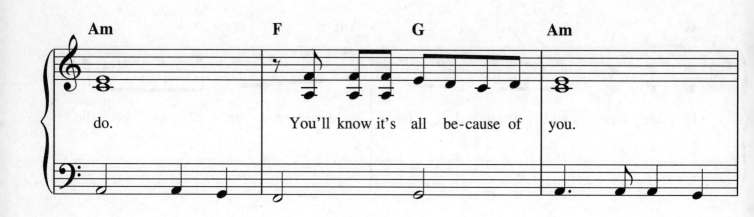

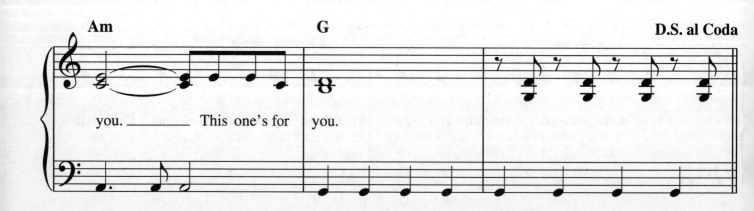

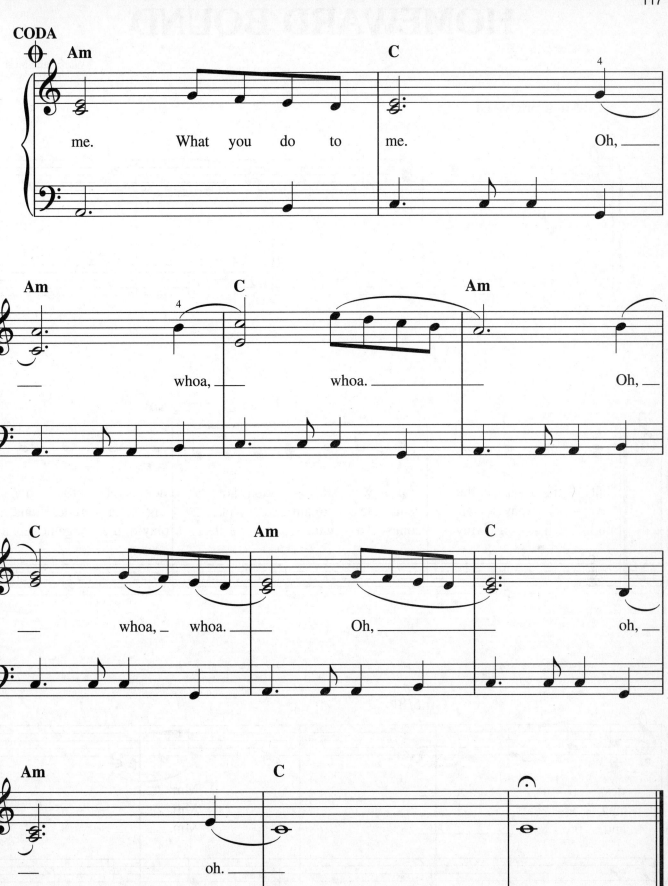

HOMEWARD BOUND

Words and Music by
PAUL SIMON

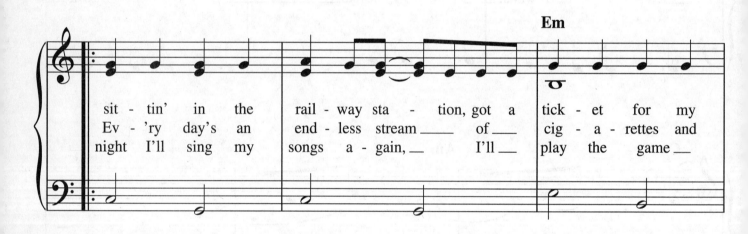

sit - tin' in the rail - way sta - tion, got a tick - et for my
Ev - 'ry day's an end - less stream ___ of ___ cig - a - rettes and
night I'll sing my songs a - gain, ___ I'll ___ play the game ___

des - ti - na - tion. ___ Mm.
mag - a - zines. ___ Mm.
and pre - tend. ___ Mm.

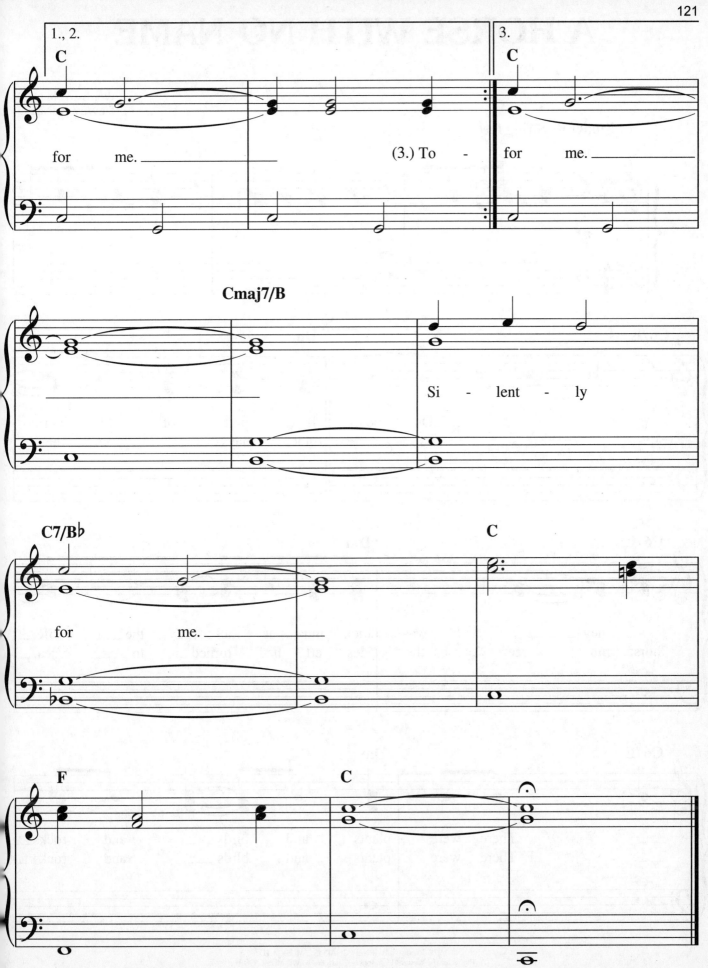

A HORSE WITH NO NAME

Words and Music by
DEWEY BUNNELL

C6/E ... and things, __ there were | **Dm** sand and hills __ and rings. __
... and things, __ there were | sand and hills __ and rings. __

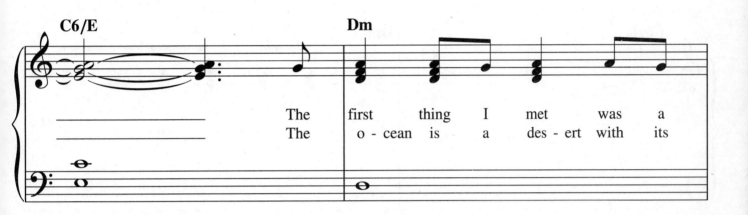

C6/E _____ The | **Dm** first thing I met was a
_____ The | o - cean is a des - ert with its

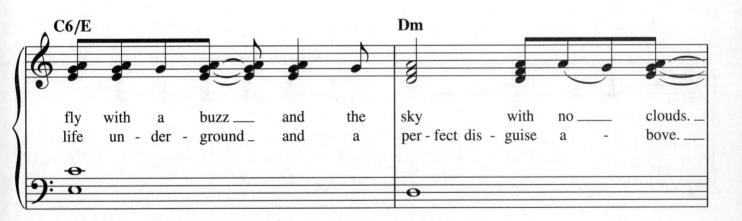

C6/E fly with a buzz __ and the | **Dm** sky with no __ clouds. __
life un - der - ground __ and a | per - fect dis - guise a - bove. __

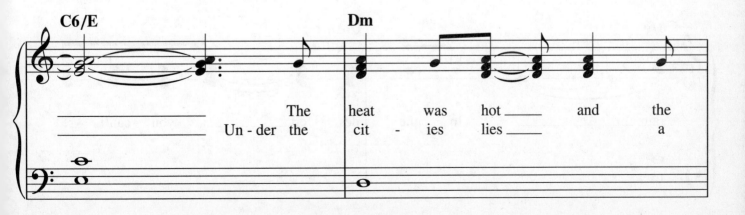

C6/E _____ The | **Dm** heat was hot ____ and the
_____ Un - der the | cit - ies lies ____ a

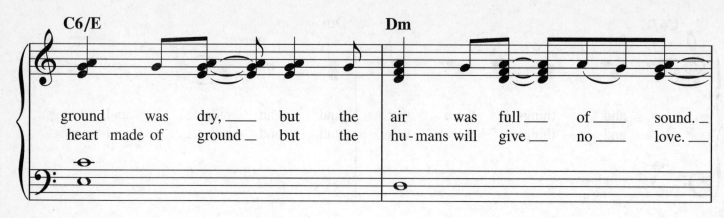

ground was dry, _____ but the air was full _____ of _____ sound. _____
heart made of ground _ but the hu-mans will give _____ no _____ love. _____

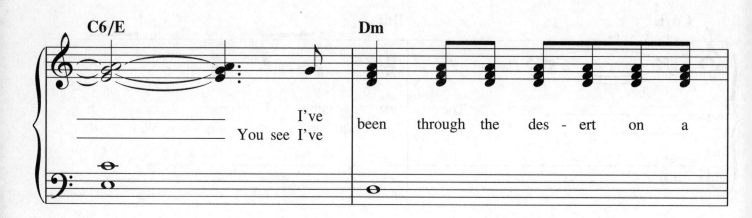

_____ I've
_____ You see I've been through the des - ert on a

horse with no name. _ It felt good to be out _____ of the

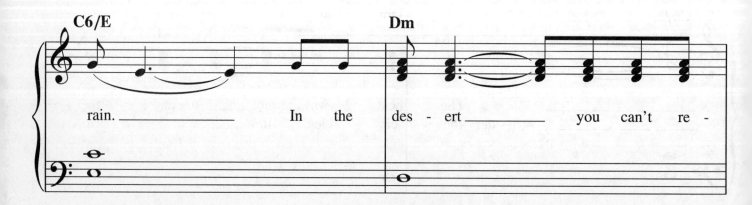

rain. _____ In the des - ert _____ you can't re -

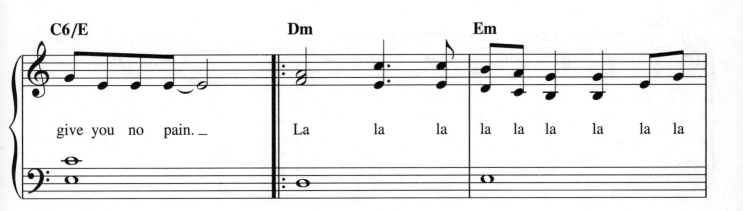

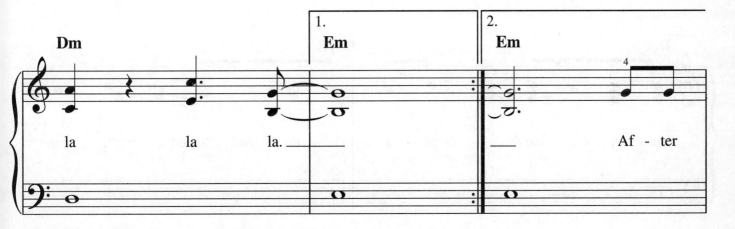

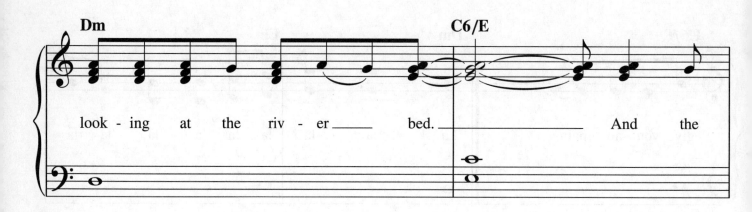

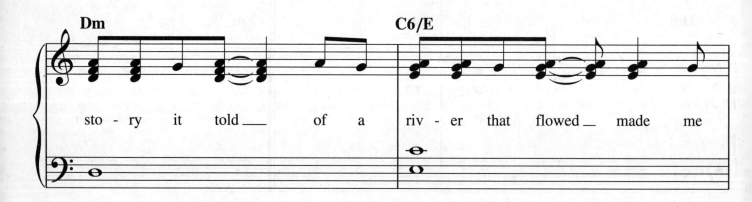

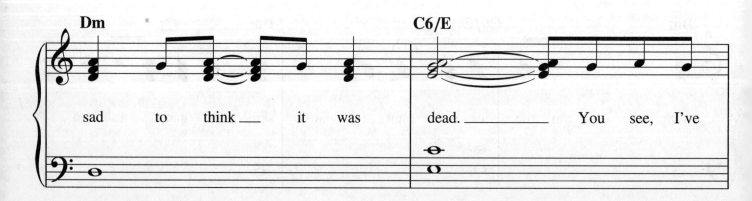

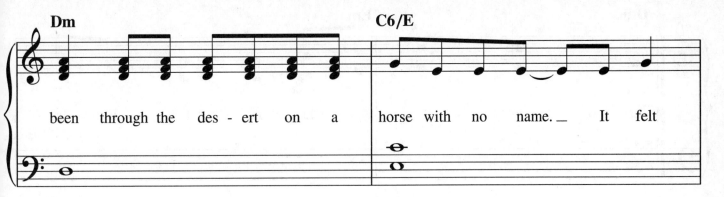

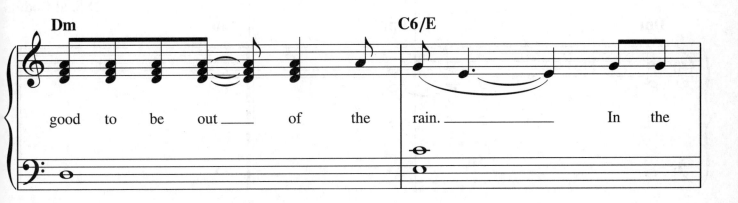

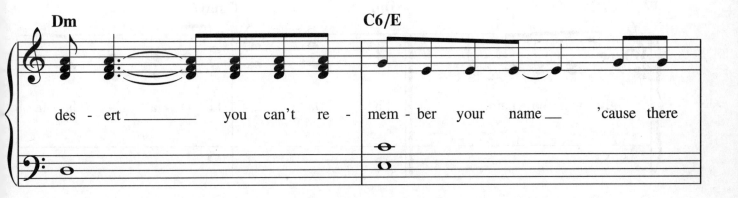

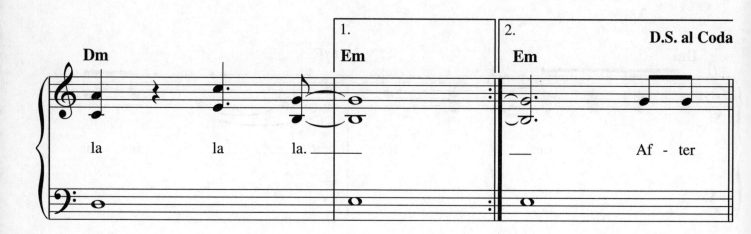

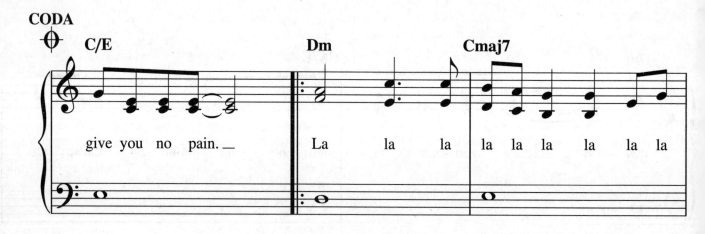

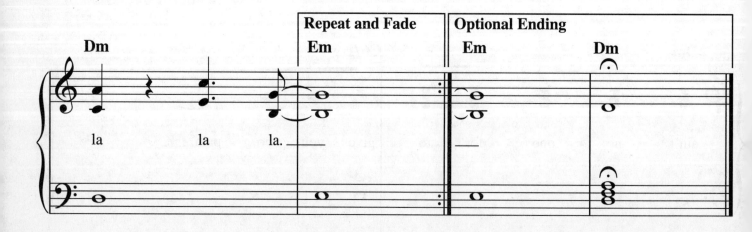

IRONIC

Lyrics by ALANIS MORISSETTE
Music by ALANIS MORISSETTE
and GLEN BALLARD

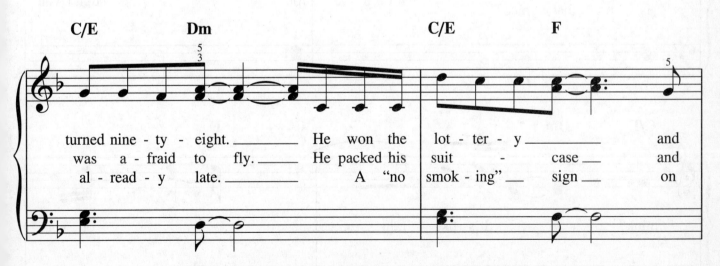

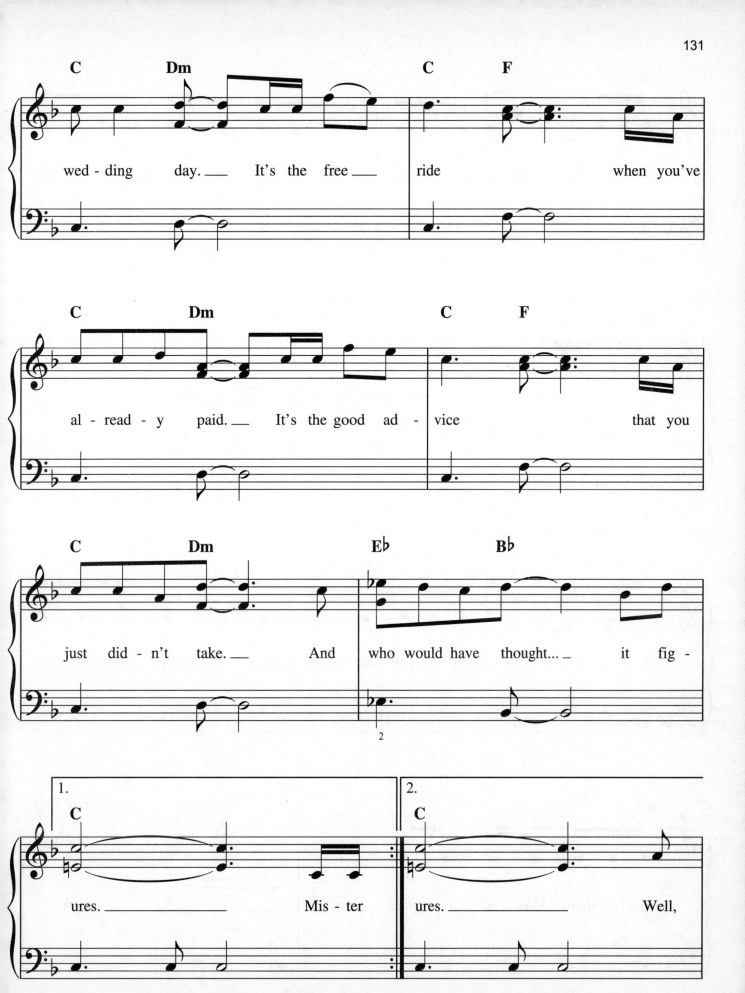

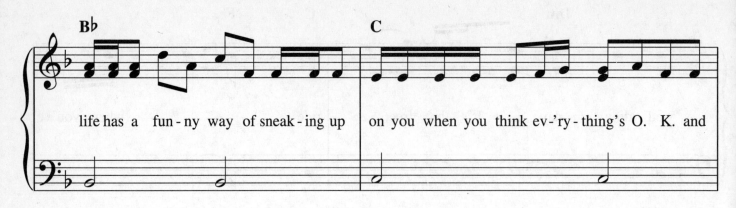

life has a fun-ny way of sneak-ing up on you when you think ev-'ry-thing's O. K. and

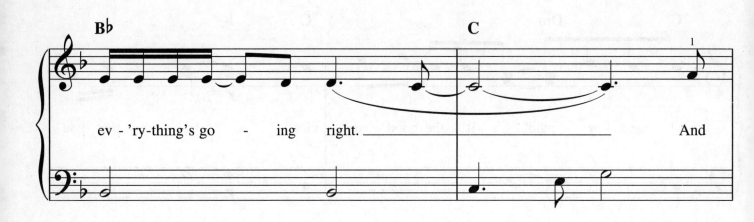

ev-'ry-thing's go - ing right. And

life has a fun-ny way of help-ing you out when you think ev-'ry-thing's gone wrong and

D.S. al Coda

ev-'ry-thing blows up in your face. A

133

CODA

meet-ing the man __ of my dreams and then meet-ing his beau-ti-ful wife. ___

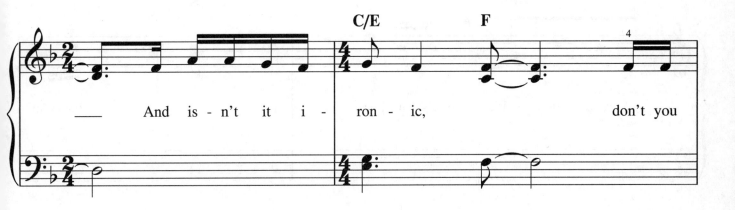

___ And is-n't it i - ron - ic, don't you

think? A lit-tle too i - ron - ic, and yeah, I

real - ly do think __ it's like rain ___ on your

wed - ding day. __ It's the free __ ride when you've

al - read - y paid. __ It's the good ad - vice that you

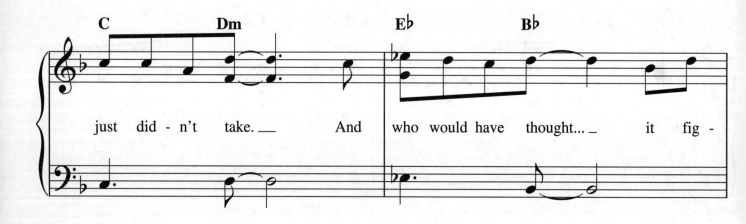

just did - n't take. __ And who would have thought... __ it fig -

ures.

And — you know life has a fun - ny way of sneak-ing up on

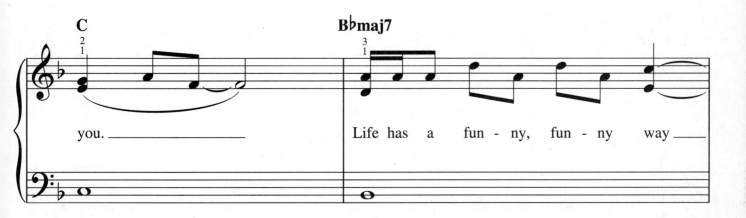

you. _____ Life has a fun - ny, fun - ny way _____

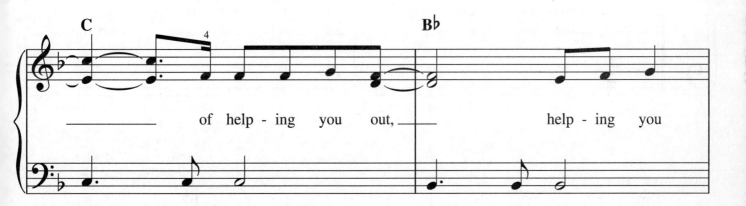

_____ of help-ing you out, _____ help - ing you

out.

I GOT A NAME

Words by NORMAN GIMBEL
Music by CHARLES FOX

Moderately, in two

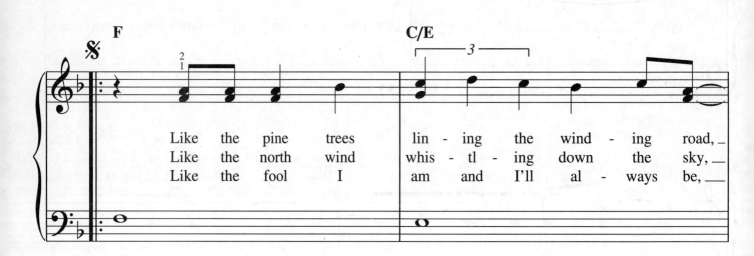

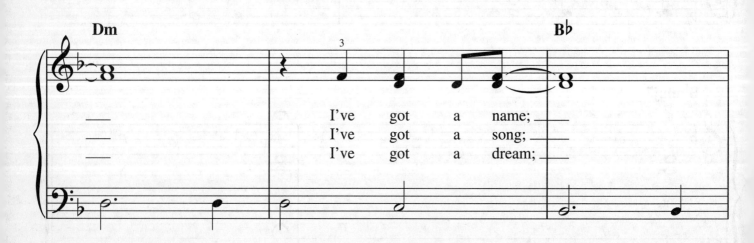

Like the pine trees lin - ing the wind - ing road, _
Like the north wind whis - tl - ing down the sky, _
Like the fool I am and I'll al - ways be, _

I've got a name; _
I've got a song; _
I've got a dream; _

And I car - ry it with___ me like my
And I car - ry it with___ me and I
Oh, I know I could share___ it if you'd

dad - dy did,___ but I'm liv - ing the dream___
sing it loud;___ if it gets me no - where,
want me to;___ if you're go - ing my way,___

that he kept hid.
I'll go there proud.
I'll go with you.

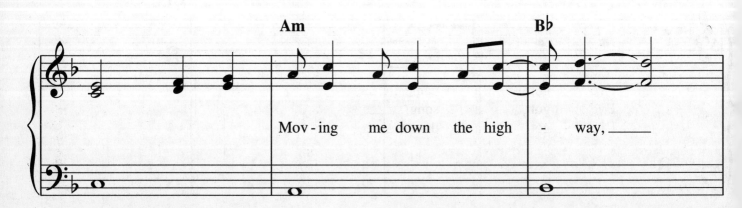

Mov - ing me down the high - way,___

roll - ing   me down   the high - way,____   mov - ing   a - head   so   life

____   won't   pass ____ me   by.

Instrumental

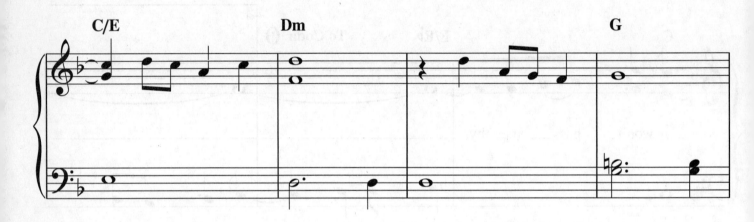

Instrumental ends   And I'm gon - na

D.S. al Coda

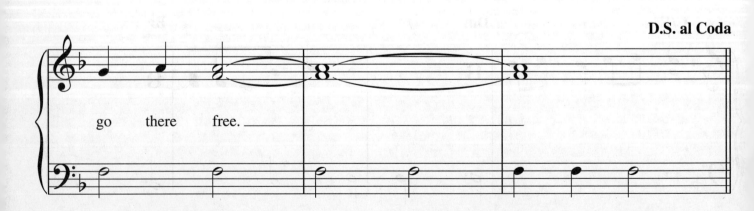

go   there   free. _____

CODA

Mov - ing me down the high - way,

roll - ing me down the high - way, mov - ing a - head so life

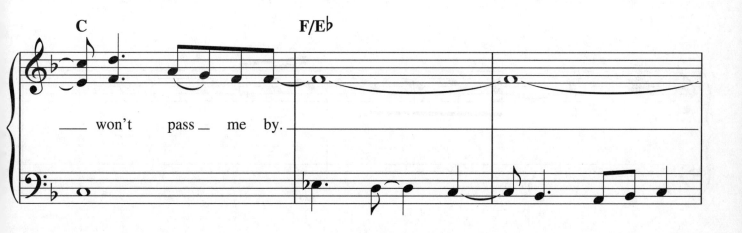

won't pass me by.

INTO THE MYSTIC

Words and Music by
VAN MORRISON

We were born be-fore the wind, ___

feel the sky, let your soul and

spir - it fly_____ in - to the mys - tic._____

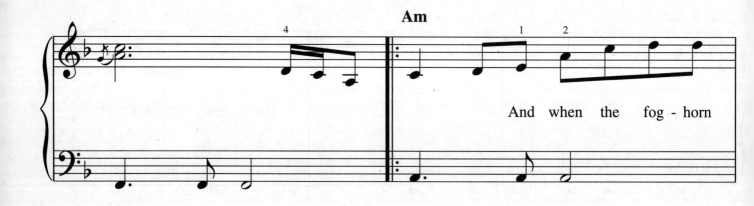

And when the fog - horn

blows,_____ I will be com - ing home. __

And when that fog - horn

blows, _____ I wan - na hear it.

I don't have to fear it, and I wan - na rock your ____

gyp - sy soul, ____ just like way back in the

days of old.____

And mag - ni - fi - cent - ly we will
And to - geth - er we will flow____

flow ____ in - to the mys - tic. ____ *Instrumental*

LEADER OF THE BAND

Words and Music by
DAN FOGELBERG

An on - ly child a - lone __
A qui - et man of mu -

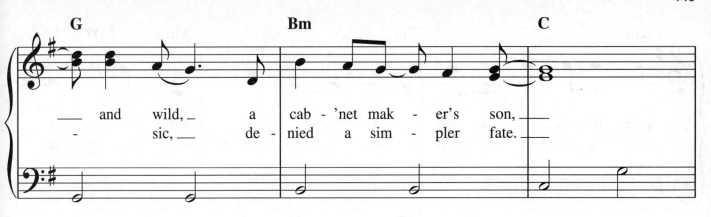

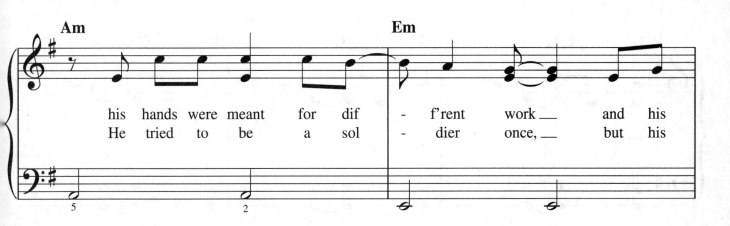

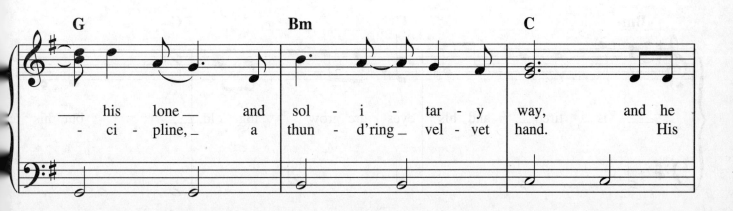

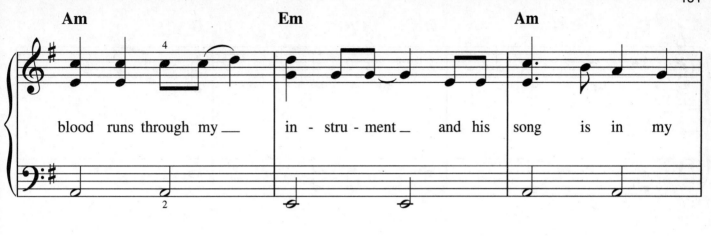

blood runs through my ___ in - stru - ment ___ and his song is in my

soul. _____ My life has been a poor ___ at - tempt ___

to im - i - tate the man. ___ I'm just a liv - ing leg -

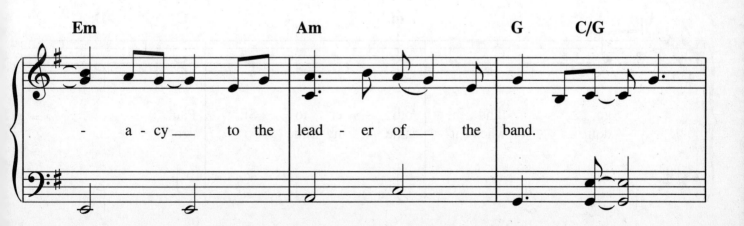

- a - cy ___ to the lead - er of ___ the band.

My broth-er's lives were dif - f'rent ____ for they
I thank you for the mu - sic ____ and your

heard an-oth-er call; ____ one went to Chi - ca-
sto - ries of the road. ____ I thank you for the free -

- go, ___ and the oth - er to St. Paul.
- dom ___ when it came my time to go.

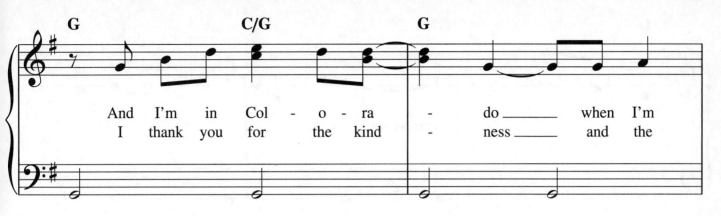

G   C/G   G

And I'm in Col - o - ra - do _____ when I'm
I thank you for the kind - ness _____ and the

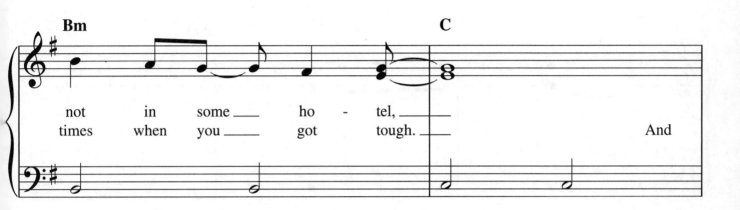

Bm   C

not in some _____ ho - tel, _____
times when you _____ got tough. _____ And

Am   Em

liv - ing out _____ this life _____ I've chose _____ and
Pa - pa, I _____ don't think _____ I said, _____ "I

Am   D7   **To Coda** ⊕ G   C/G

come to know so well.
love you" near e -

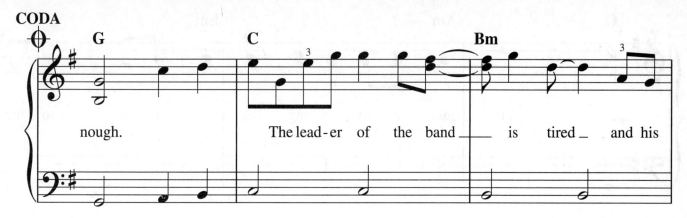

nough. The lead-er of the band___ is tired__ and his

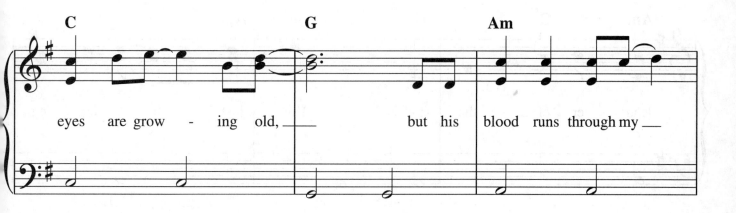

eyes are grow - ing old, ___ but his blood runs through my ___

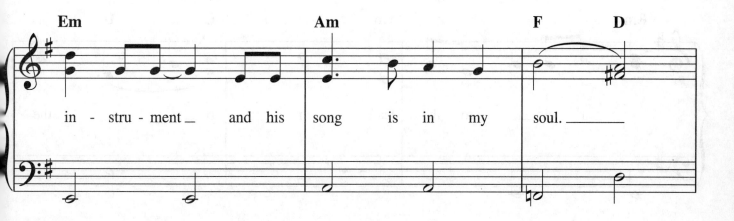

in - stru - ment __ and his song is in my soul. _____

My life has been a poor___ at - tempt_ to im - i - tate the man._

I'm just a liv - ing leg - a - cy ___ to the

lead - er of ___ the band. I'm just a liv - ing leg -

- a - cy ___ to the lead - er of _____ the

band. ___

LEARNING TO FLY

Words and Music by TOM PETTY
and JEFF LYNNE

LIKE THE WAY I DO

Words and Music by
MELISSA ETHERIDGE

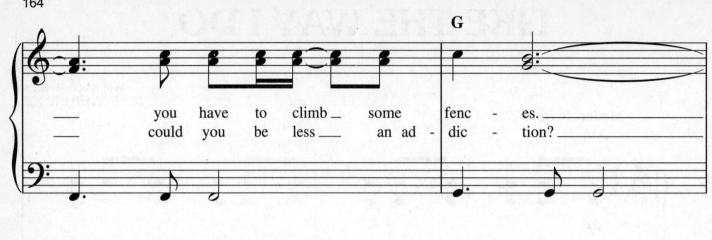

you have to climb — some fenc - es. _____

could you be less — an ad - dic - tion? _____

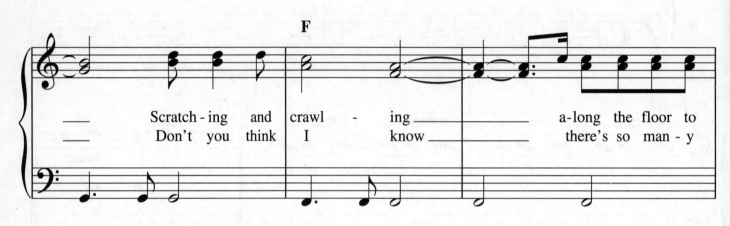

Scratch - ing and crawl - ing _____ a-long the floor to

Don't you think I know _____ there's so man - y

touch you, _____ and just when it feels right

oth - ers _____ who would beg, steal and lie, fight, kill and

you say you found some-one — to hold you. Does she

die just — to hold you, hold you

want you, in - fat - u - ate and haunt you?__ Does she know just how to

shock you,__ e - lec - tri - fy and rock you?_____ Does she in -

To Coda ⊕

ject you, se - duce you and af - fect you _____ like the way I do,

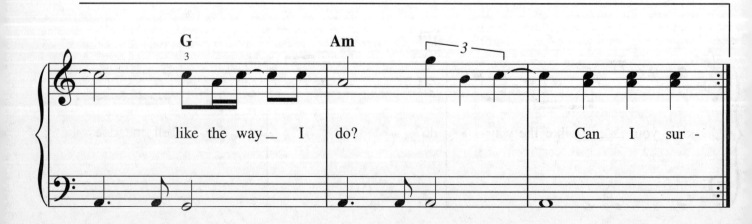

like the way_ I do? Can I sur -

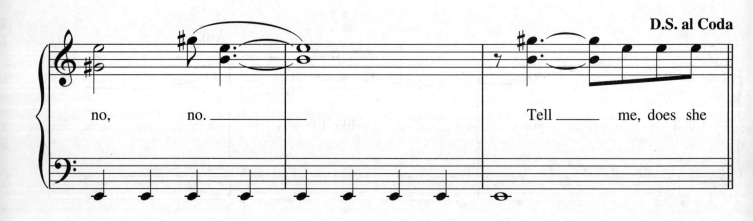

do? *(Vocal 1st time only)*

LET HER CRY

Words and Music by DARIUS CARLOS RUCKER,
EVERETT DEAN FELBER, MARK WILLIAM BRYAN
and JAMES GEORGE SONEFELD

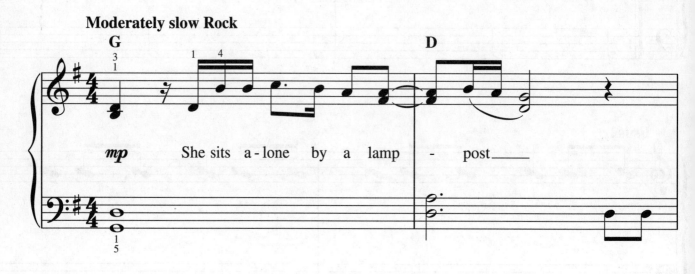

She sits a-lone by a lamp - post

try'n't to find a thought that's es - caped her mind.

She says, "Dad's the one I love the most,

C(add9) / **G**

pray to God_ you got-ta help me fly_ a - way._ And just
sat back down,_ had a beer_ and felt sor-ry for my- self. Say - in', let her
"Oh, ma - ma,_ please help me._Won't you hold my_ hand?" And

C(add9) / **G**

cry if the tears_ fall down like rain._ Let her

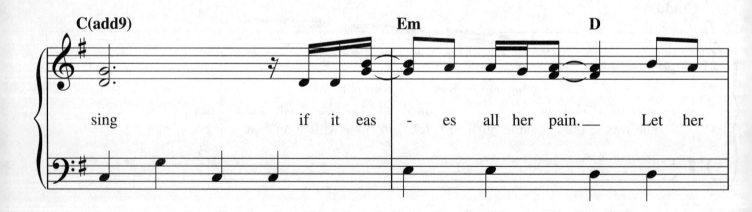

C(add9) / **Em** / **D**

sing if it eas - es all her pain._ Let her

C(add9) / **G**

go, let her walk_ right out on_ me._ And if the

LOSING MY RELIGION

Words and Music by WILLIAM BERRY,
PETER BUCK, MICHAEL MILLS
and MICHAEL STIPE

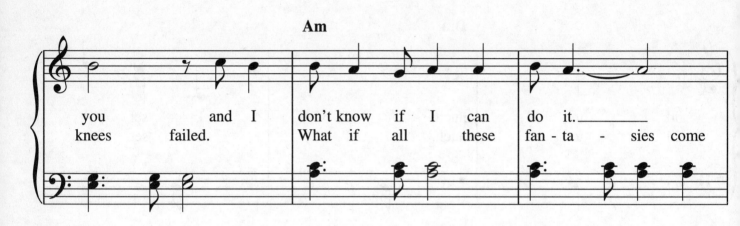

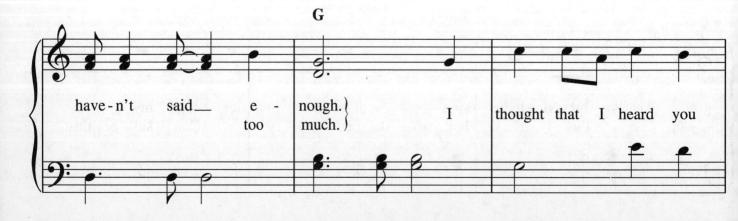

laugh - ing. _____ I thought that I heard you sing. _____

_____ I think I thought I saw you

try. Ev - er - y

But that was just a dream.

MRS. ROBINSON

Words and Music by
PAUL SIMON

D.S. al Coda
(with repeat)

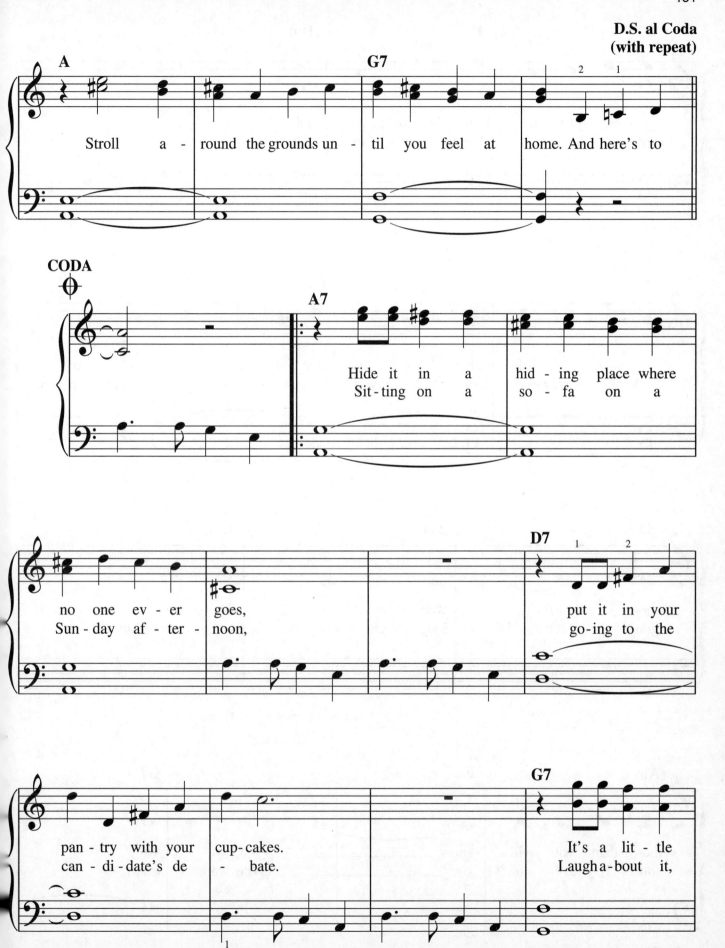

Stroll a - round the grounds un - til you feel at home. And here's to

CODA

Hide it in a hid - ing place where
Sit - ting on a so - fa on a

no one ev - er goes, put it in your
Sun - day af - ter - noon, go - ing to the

pan - try with your cup - cakes. It's a lit - tle
can - di - date's de - bate. Laugh a - bout it,

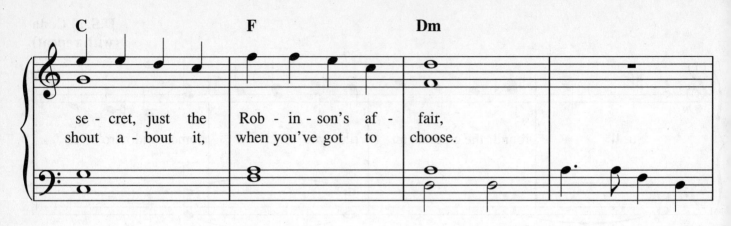

se - cret, just the Rob - in - son's af - fair,
shout a - bout it, when you've got to choose.

most of all, you've got to hide it from the kids. Coo, coo, ca -
Ev -'ry way you look at it, you lose. Where have you

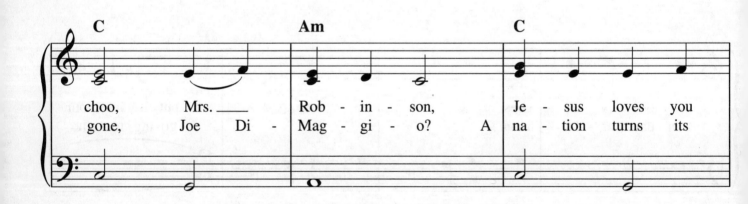

choo, Mrs. ___ Rob - in - son, Je - sus loves you
gone, Joe Di - Mag - gi - o? A na - tion turns its

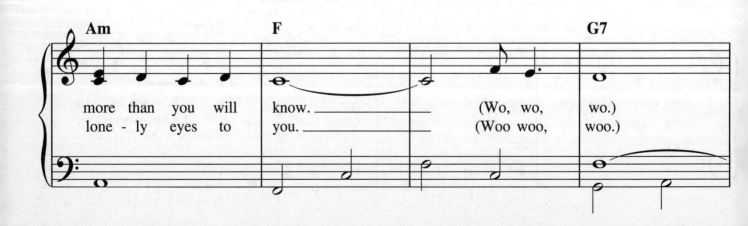

more than you will know. ___ (Wo, wo, wo.)
lone - ly eyes to you. ___ (Woo woo, woo.)

God bless you, please,   Mrs. ___ Rob - in - son,
What's that you say,   Mrs. ___ Rob - in - son,

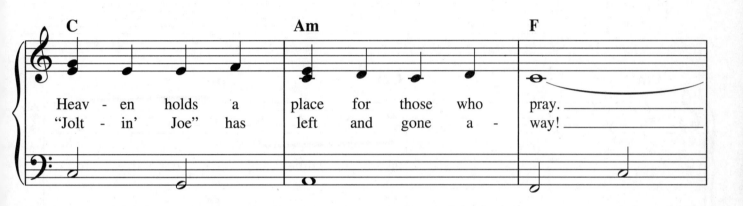

Heav - en holds a place for those who pray. _____
"Jolt - in' Joe" has left and gone a - way! _____

___ (Hey, hey, hey. _____ ___ hey, hey, hey.)
___ (Hey, hey, hey. _____ ___ hey, hey, hey.)

LOVE OF A LIFETIME

Words and Music by BILL LEVERTY
and CARL SNARE

know our dreams can all come true with love that we can

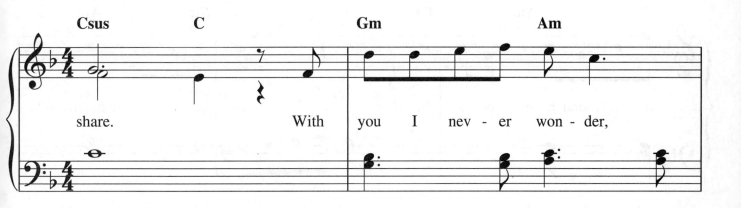

share. With you I nev-er won-der,

"Will you be there for me?" With you I nev-er won-der. You're the

right one for me. I fi-n'lly found the love of a

life-time, a love to last my whole life through. I

fi-n'lly found the love of a life-time, for - ev - er in my heart. I

To Coda ⊕

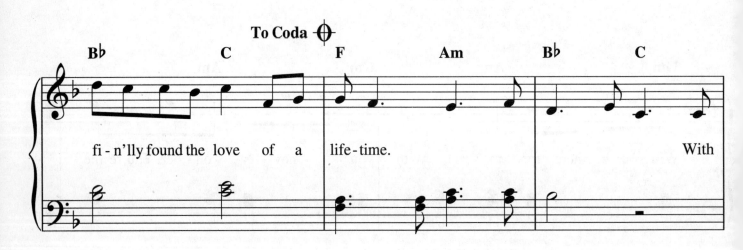

fi - n'lly found the love of a life-time. With

ev - 'ry kiss our love is like brand - new, and

ev - 'ry star up in the sky was made for me and you.

Still, we both know that the road is long, but we

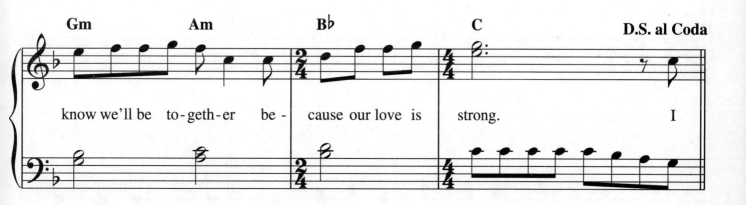

know we'll be to-geth-er be- cause our love is strong. I

life - time.

LYIN' EYES

Words and Music by DON HENLEY
and GLENN FREY

Cit - y   girls __   just
She gets   up __   and

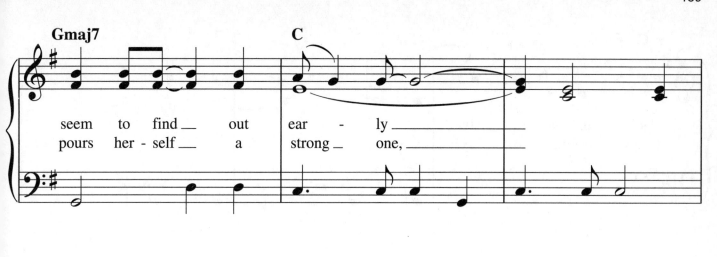

seem to find out ear - ly
pours her-self a strong one,

how to o - pen doors with just a smile.
and stares out at the stars up in the sky.

A rich old man, and she won't have to
An - oth - er night, it's gon - na be a

wor - ry.
long one.

She'll dress up all in
She draws the shade and

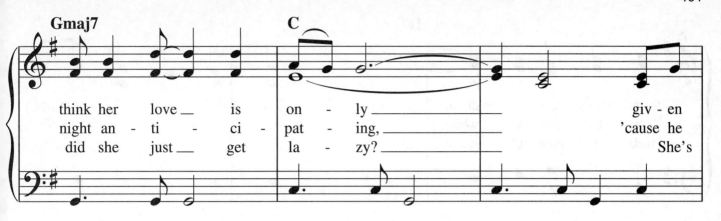

Gmaj7 — **C**

think her love is on - ly giv - en
night an - ti - ci - pat - ing, 'cause he
did she just get la - zy? She's

Am — **C** — **G**

to a man with hands as cold as ice.
makes her feel the way she used to feel.
so far gone, she feels just like a fool.

C — **D** — **G** — **Gmaj7**

So she tells him she must go out for the
She rush - es to his arms, they fall to -
My, oh my, you sure know how to ar -

C/E — **C** — **Bm7** — **Am**

eve - ning
geth - er. She whis - pers that it's
range things. You set it up so

to com - fort an old

MEET VIRGINIA

Words and Music by PAT MONAHAN,
JAMES STAFFORD and ROB HOTCHKISS

She nev - er com - pro - mis - es,
Well, here she is a - gain on the

loves ba - bies and ___ sur - pris - es, wears high heels when she
phone. Just like me, hates to be a - lone. We just

ex - er - cis - es. Ain't that beau - ti - ful? ___
like to sit home and rip on the pres - i - dent.

Meet Vir - gin - ia.

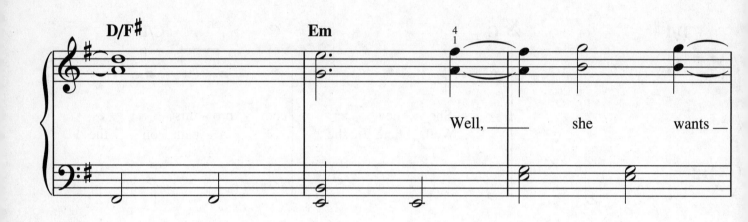

Well, _____ she wants _____

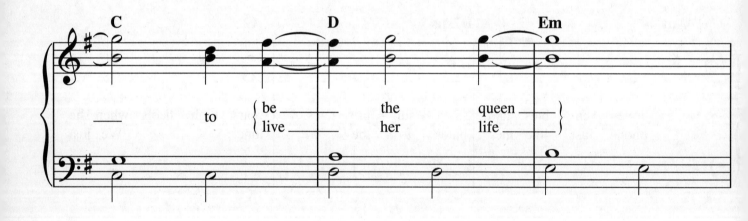

_____ to { be _____ the queen _____ }
{ live _____ her life _____ }

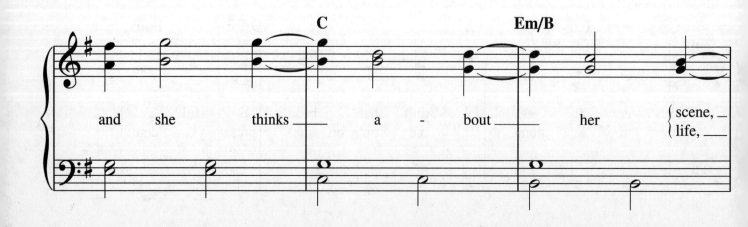

and she thinks _____ a - bout _____ her { scene, _____
{ life, _____

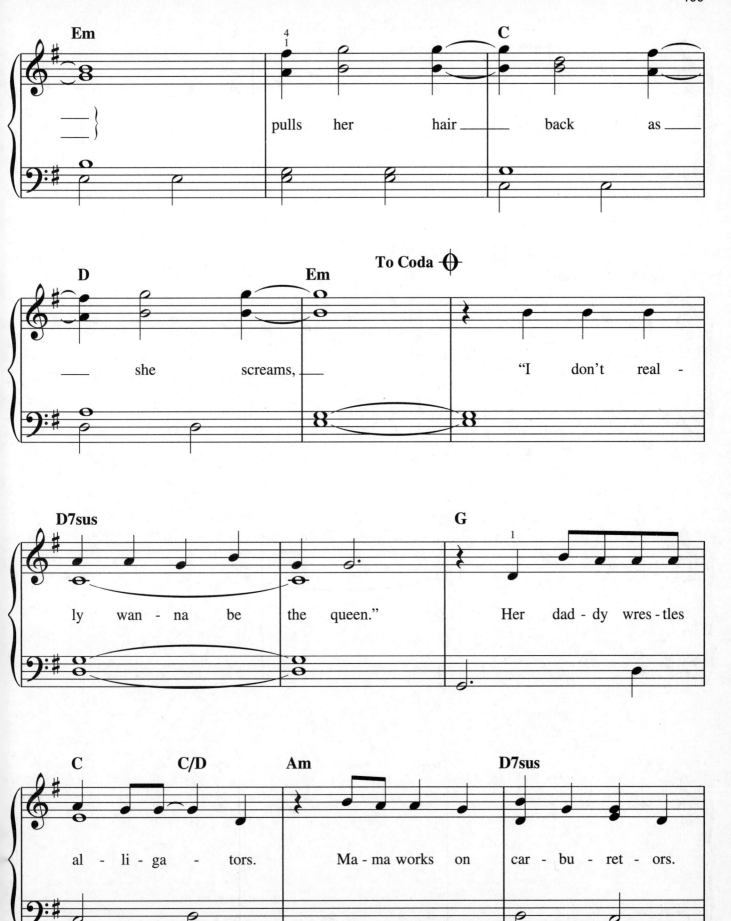

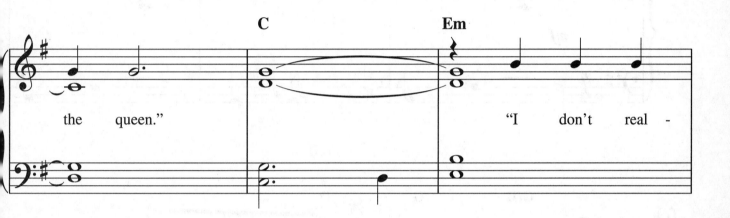

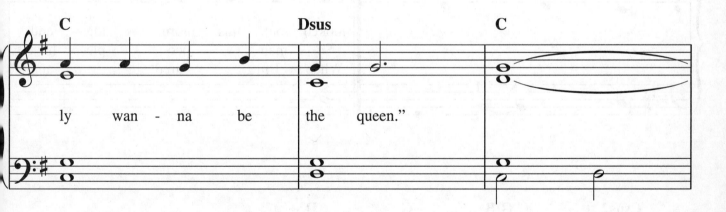

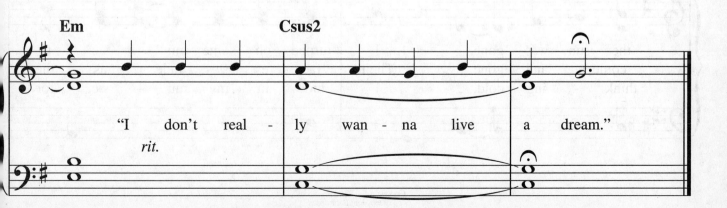

MORE THAN A FEELING

Words and Music by
TOM SCHOLZ

I
looked out this morn - ing and
So man - y peo - ple have
When I'm____ tired____ and

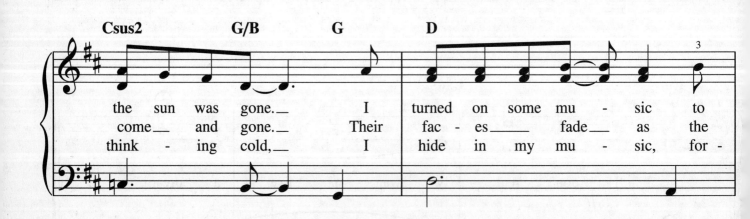

the sun was gone.____ I turned on some mu - sic to
come____ and gone.____ Their fac - es____ fade____ as the
think - ing cold,____ I hide in my mu - sic, for -

start my day._ I lost my-self_ in a fa- mil-iar song. I
years go by,_ yet I still re-call_ as I wan-der on, as
get the day,_ and dream of a girl_ I used to know. I

closed my_ eyes_ and I slipped a-way._
clear as the sun_ in the sum-mer sky._
closed my_ eyes_ and she slipped a-way._

It's

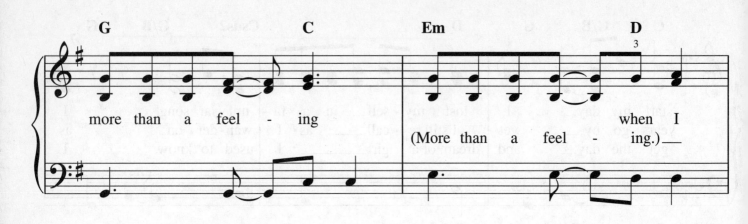

more than a feel - ing
(More than a feel - ing.) when I

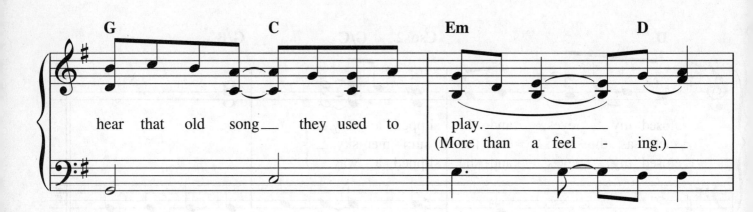

hear that old song they used to play.
(More than a feel - ing.)

To Coda ⊕

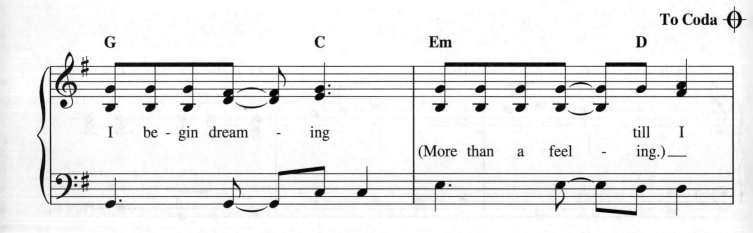

I be - gin dream - ing
(More than a feel - ing.) till I

see Mar - i - anne walk a - way.
I see my

Mar - i - anne walk - in' a - way.

D.S. al Coda

NEVER GOING BACK AGAIN

Words and Music by
LINDSEY BUCKINGHAM

Pop Ballad

She broke   down _   and
You don't   know _   what it

let   me _   in. _
means   to _   win. _

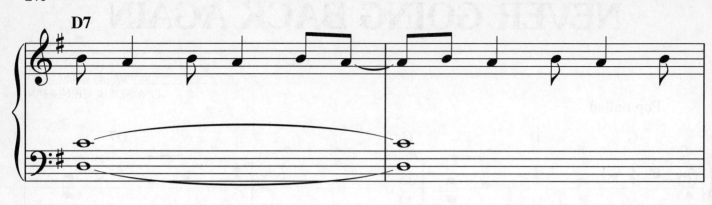

Made me ___ see
Come 'round ___ and

where I've ___ been. ___
see me a - gain. ___

PATIENCE

Words and Music by W. AXL ROSE,
SLASH, IZZY STRADLIN', DUFF McKAGAN
and STEVEN ADLER

All we need___ is just___ a lit - tle pa - tience."

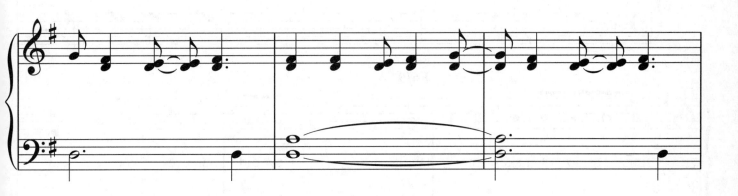

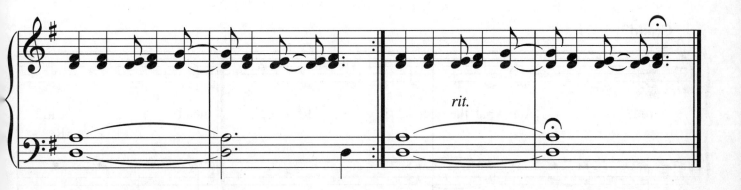

rit.

Additional Lyrics

2. I sit here on the stairs 'cause I'd rather be alone.
   If I can't have you right now, I'll wait, dear.
   Sometimes I get so tense but I can't speed up the time.
   But you know, love, there's one more thing to consider:

   Said, "Woman, take it slow, and things will be just fine.
   You and I'll just use a little patience."
   Said, "Sugar, take the time 'cause the lights are shining bright.
   You and I've got what it takes to make it.
   We won't fake it, ah, I'll never break it 'cause I can't take it."

PHOTOGRAPH

Lyrics by CHAD KROEGER
Music by NICKELBACK

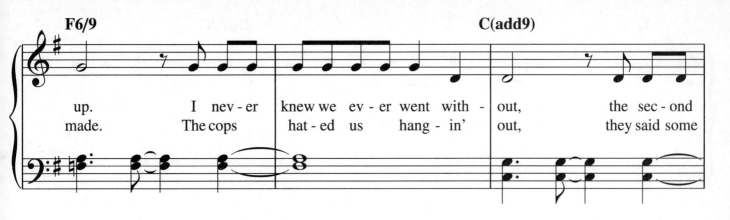

up.   I nev - er knew we ev - er went with - out,   the sec - ond
made.   The cops hat - ed us hang - in' out,   they said some

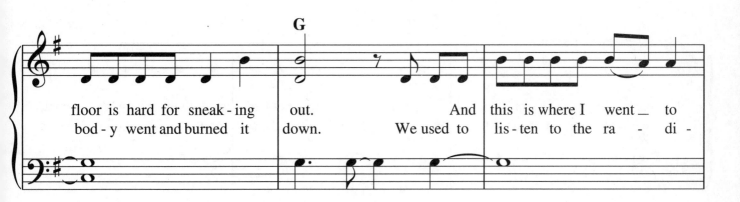

floor is hard for sneak - ing out.   And this is where I went __ to
bod - y went and burned it down.   We used to lis - ten to the ra - di -

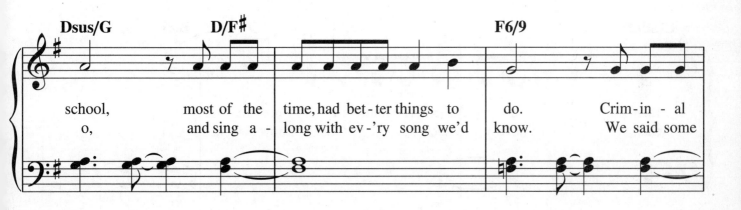

school,   most of the time, had bet - ter things to do.   Crim - in - al
o,   and sing a - long with ev - 'ry song we'd know.   We said some

rec - ord says I broke in twice,   I must have done it half a doz - en
day we'd find out how it feels   to sing to more than just the steer - ing

times. I won-der if it's __ too late, should I go
wheel. Kim's the first girl __ I kissed, I was so

back and try to grad-u - ate? Life's bet - ter now than it was __ back
ner-vous that I near - ly missed. She's had a cou - ple of kids __ since

then, if I was them, I would-n't let me in. __   Oh, __
then, I have-n't seen her since God __ knows when. __

whoa, __ whoa, oh, God, I, __ I. Ev - 'ry

221

mem-o-ry of look-ing out the | back door, I had the | pho-to al-bum spread out on the

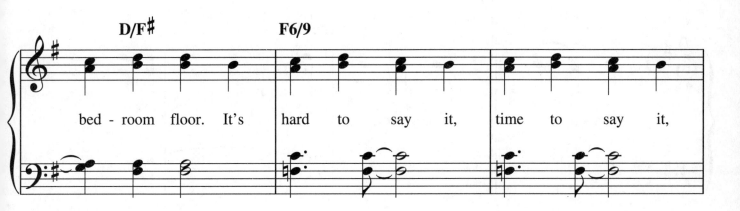

bed-room floor. It's | hard to say it, | time to say it,

good - bye, ___ | good - bye. Ev-'ry | mem-o-ry of walk-ing out the

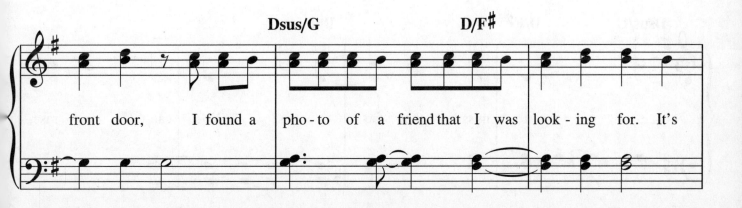

front door, I found a | pho-to of a friend that I was | look-ing for. It's

222

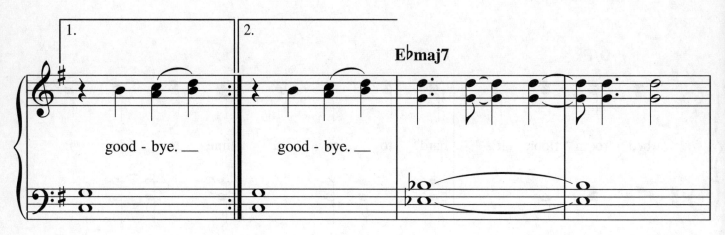

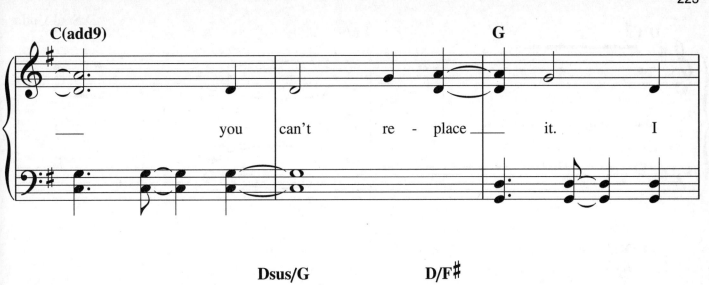

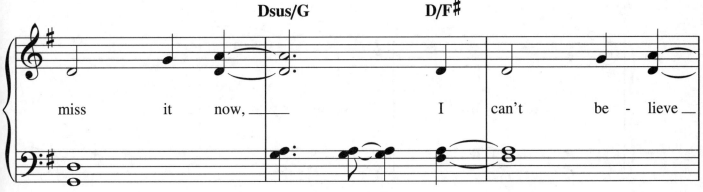

D.S. al Coda

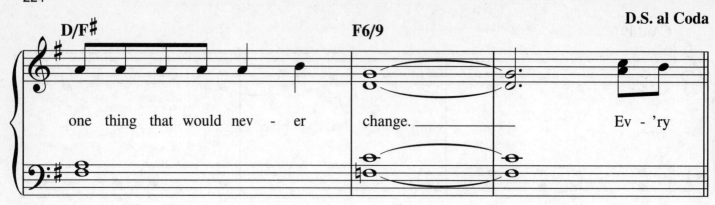

one thing that would nev - er change._____ Ev - 'ry

good - bye,___ good - bye,_____

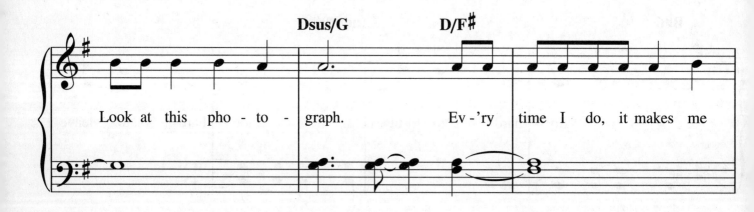

Look at this pho - to - graph. Ev -'ry time I do, it makes me

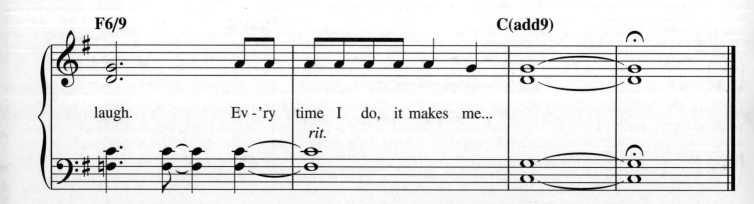

laugh. Ev -'ry time I do, it makes me...

REDEMPTION SONG

Words and Music by
BOB MARLEY

Moderately, Folk style

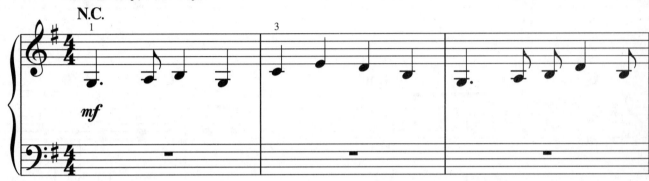

Old pi - rates, yes, they rob
pate your - selves from men - tal

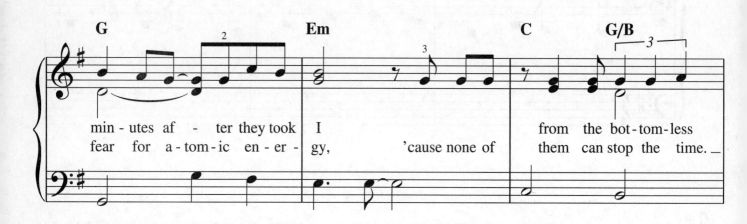

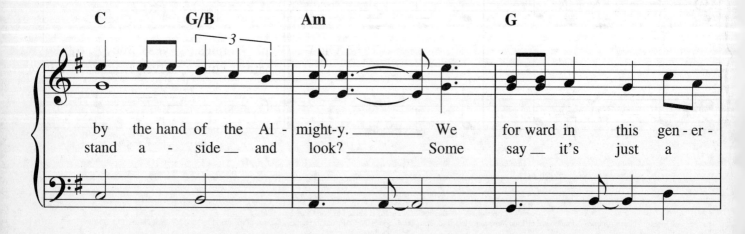

227

SHE TALKS TO ANGELS

Words and Music by CHRIS ROBINSON
and RICH ROBINSON

(1.,3.) She paints her eyes as black as night, now.
pock - et.

Pulls those shades _ down _ tight.
She wears a cross a - round her neck.

Yeah, _ she gives a smile _ when the
Yes, _ the _ hair is from a

She keeps a lock of hair in her

She — don't know no lov - er,

none that I ev - er seen. _____ And to her __ that ain't noth-

in', but to me it means, _____ means ev - 'ry -

SMALL TOWN

Words and Music by
JOHN MELLENCAMP

1. Well, I was born in a small ___ town,
2. (See additional lyrics)

and I live in a small ___ town;

prob'ly die in a small ___ town.

Oh, those small ___ com-mun-i-ties.

C   G/C   F/C   G/C

___ town, ___   still hay-seed e-nough to say,   "Look who's in the big town."

C   G/B   F/A   G   Dm

But my bed is in a   small town; oh, and that's   good e - nough ___ for

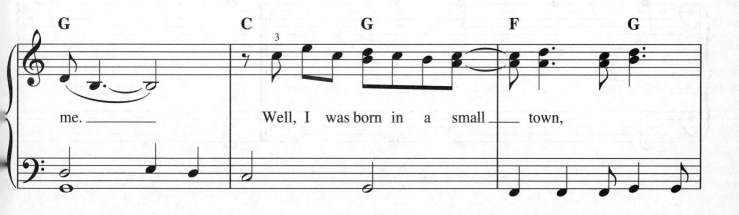

G   C   G   F   G

me. _____   Well, I was born in a small ___ town,

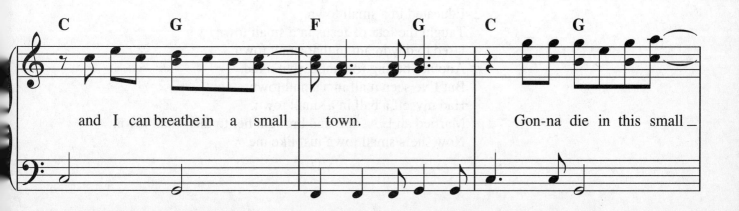

C   G   F   G   C   G

and I can breathe in a small ___ town.   Gon-na die in this small ___

Additional Lyrics

2. Educated in a small town,
Taught the fear of Jesus in a small town;
Used to daydream in that small town.
Another boring romantic, that's me.
But I've seen it all in a small town,
Had myself a ball in a small town.
Married an L.A. doll and brought her to this small town,
Now she's small town just like me.

STRONG ENOUGH

Words and Music by KEVIN GILBERT,
DAVID BAERWALD, SHERYL CROW,
BRIAN McLEOD, BILL BOTTRELL
and DAVID RICKETTS

1.God, I feel like hell to - night, the
2.- 4. *(See additional lyrics)*

tears of rage I can - not fight. I'd be the last to help you un - der-

stand. Are you strong e - nough to be my man? My

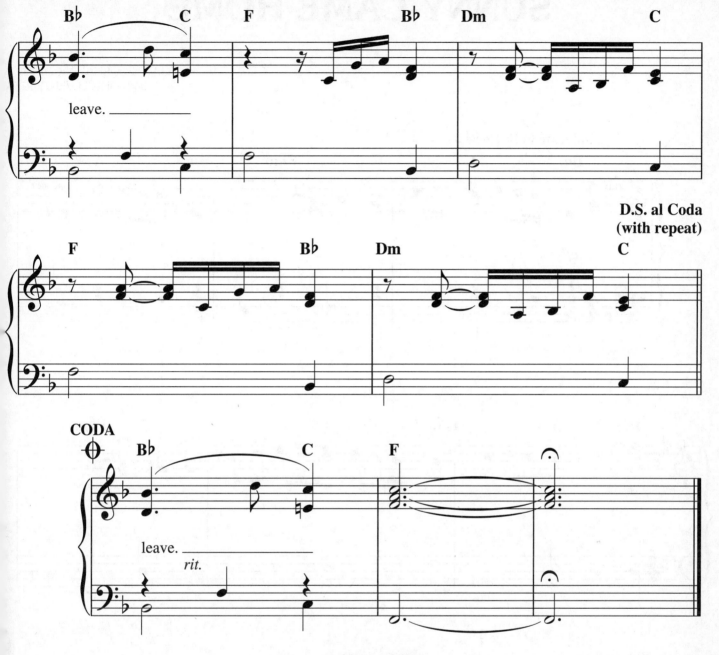

Additional Lyrics

2. Nothing's true and nothing's right,
   So let me be alone tonight.
   You can't change the way I am.
   Are you strong enough to be my man?

3. I have a face I cannot show,
   I make the rules up as I go.
   It's try and love me if you can.
   Are you strong enough to be my man?

4. When I've shown you that I just don't care,
   When I'm throwing punches in the air,
   When I'm broken down and cannot stand,
   Will you be strong enough to be my man?

SUNNY CAME HOME

Words and Music by SHAWN COLVIN
and JOHN LEVENTHAL

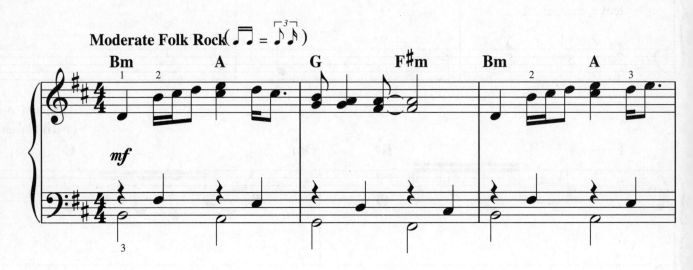

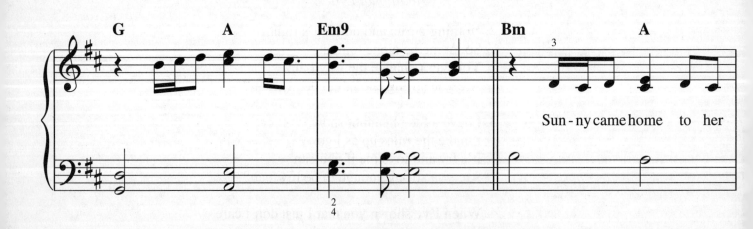

Sun - ny came home to her

248

TAKE ME HOME, COUNTRY ROADS

Words and Music by JOHN DENVER,
BILL DANOFF and TAFFY NIVERT

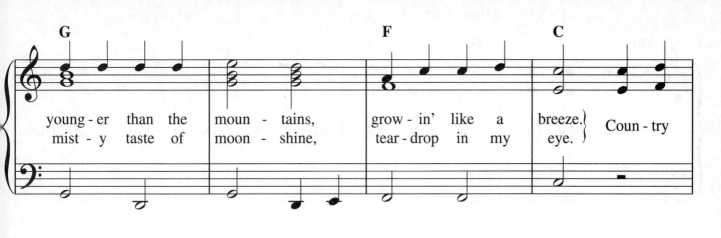

G younger than the / misty taste of / **F** grow-in' like a / tear-drop in my / **C** breeze. / eye. Coun-try
mountains, / moonshine,

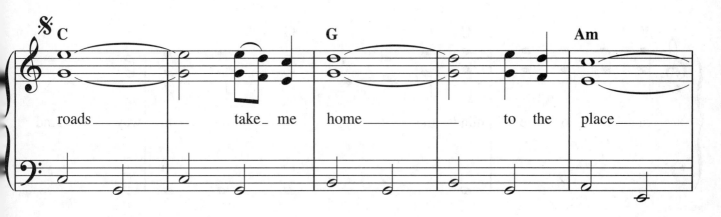

C roads ____ take_ me **G** home ____ to the **Am** place ____

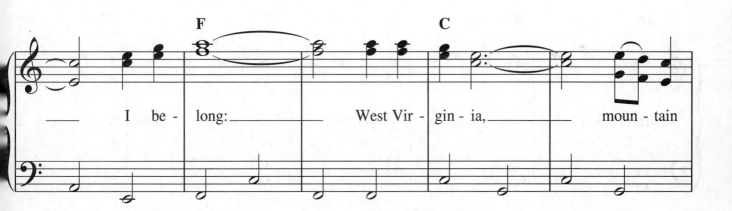

____ I be- **F** long: ____ West Vir - gin- ia, **C** ____ moun - tain

To Coda

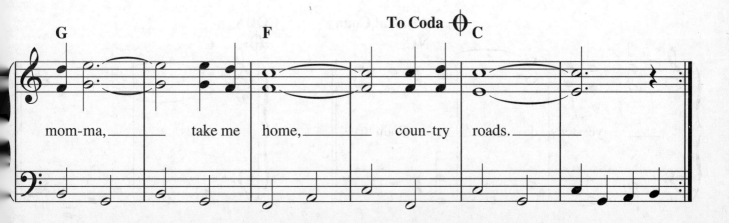

G mom-ma, ____ **F** take me home, ____ **C** coun-try roads. ____

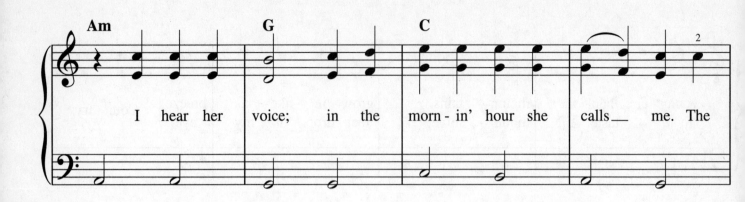

I hear her voice; in the morn-in' hour she calls___ me. The

ra-di-o re-minds me of my home far a-way. And

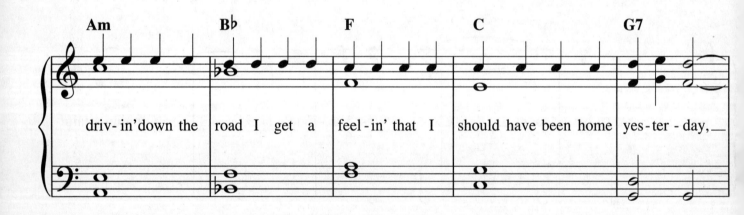

driv-in'down the road I get a feel-in' that I should have been home yes-ter-day,

___ yes-ter-day.___ Coun-try

roads.___

THE WEIGHT

By J.R. ROBERTSON

1. I pulled in - to Na - za - reth, __ was feel - in' 'bout half - past dead.

2.–5. *(See additional lyrics)*

I just need some - place where I can lay my head. __

"Hey, mis - ter, can you tell me where a man might find a bed?"

Additional Lyrics

2. I picked up my bag, I went looking for a place to hide,
   When I saw Carmen and the Devil walking side by side.
   I said, "Hey, Carmen, come on, let's go downtown."
   She said, "I gotta go but my friend can stick around."
   Chorus

3. Go down, Miss Moses, there's nothing you can say.
   It's just ol' Luke, and Luke's waiting on the judgement day.
   "Well, Luke, my friend, what about young Anna Lee?"
   He said, "Do me a favour, son, won't you stay
   And keep Anna Lee company?"
   Chorus

4. Crazy Chester caught me and followed me in the fog.
   He said, "I will fix your rack if you'll take Jack, my dog."
   I said, "Wait a minute, Chester, you know I'm a peaceful man."
   He said, "That's OK, boy, won't you feed him when you can?"
   Chorus

5. Catch a cannonball now, to take me down the line.
   My bag is sinking and I do believe it's time
   To get back to Miss Fanny, you know she's the only one
   Who sent me here with her regards for everyone.
   Chorus

TAXI

Words and Music by
HARRY CHAPIN

"Oh, where ___ you go-ing to, my La-dy Blue? It's a

shame you ruined your gown ___ in the rain." She just looked ___ out the

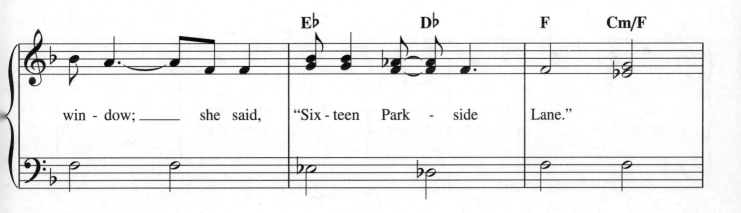

win-dow; ___ she said, "Six-teen Park-side Lane."

Some-thing a - bout __ her was fa - mil - iar. ____ I could
not __ much more __ for us to talk a - bout. What-

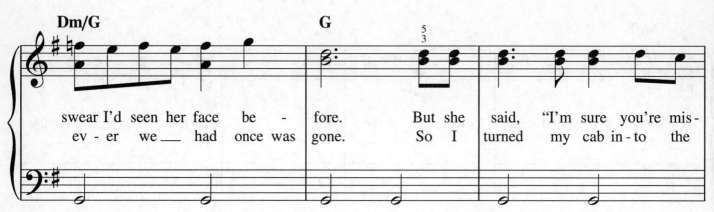

swear I'd seen her face be - fore. But she said, "I'm sure you're mis-
ev - er we __ had once was gone. So I turned my cab in - to the

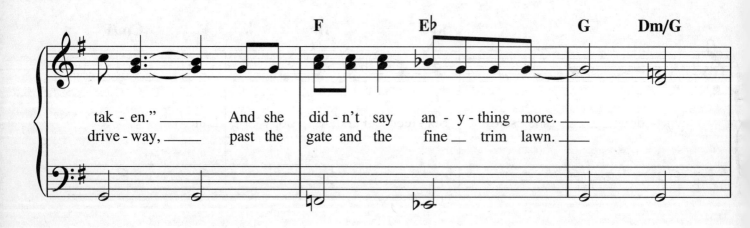

tak - en." ____ And she did - n't say an - y - thing more. __
drive - way, ____ past the gate and the fine __ trim lawn. __

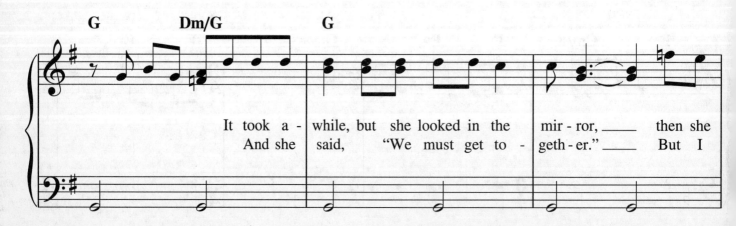

It took a - while, but she looked in the mir - ror, ____ then she
And she said, "We must get to - geth - er." ____ But I

glanced at the li - cense for my name. _____ A

knew it would nev - er be ar - ranged. Then she

To Coda ⊕

smile seemed to come to her slow - ly. _____ It was a

hand - ed me twen - ty dol - lars for a two - fif - ty fare. She said,

sad smile, _ just the same. _

And she

said, "How _ are you, Har - ry?" _ I said, "How are you, Sue? _

Through the too man-y miles __ and the too lit - tle smiles, __ I

still _____ re - mem - ber you."

It was

some - where ___ in a fair - y - tale; ___ I used to take her home in my

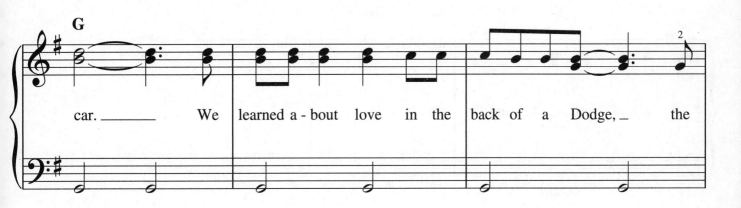

car. ___ We learned a - bout love in the back of a Dodge, _ the

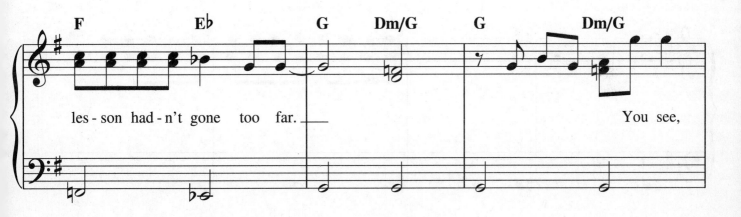

les - son had - n't gone too far. ___ You see,

she was gon - na be an ac - tress, _ and I was gon - na learn to fly. _

She took off____ to find the foot - lights;

I took off____ to find the sky.

Whoa,

I've got____ some-thing in - side____ me to drive a prin - cess
I've got____ some-thing in - side____ me, not what my life's a -

Ba - by's so

high   that she's sky - ing, _____   yes, she's

fly - ing _____   a - fraid to   fall. _____

I'll tell you why ba - by's cry - ing: ___

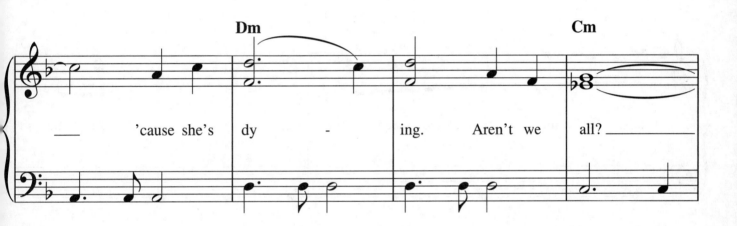

___ 'cause she's dy - ing. Aren't we all? ___

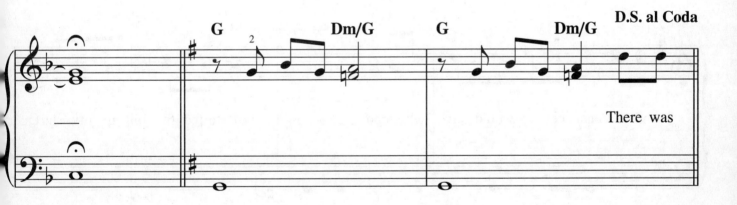

There was

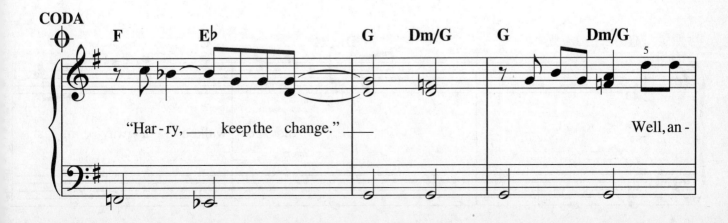

"Har - ry, ___ keep the change." ___

Well, an -

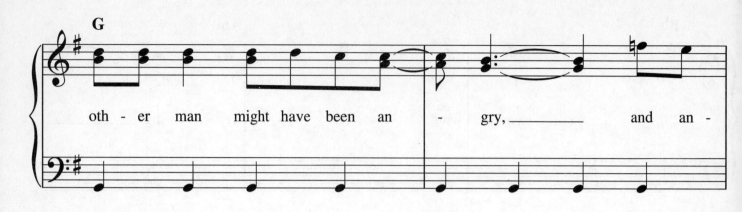

oth - er man might have been an - gry, _____ and an -

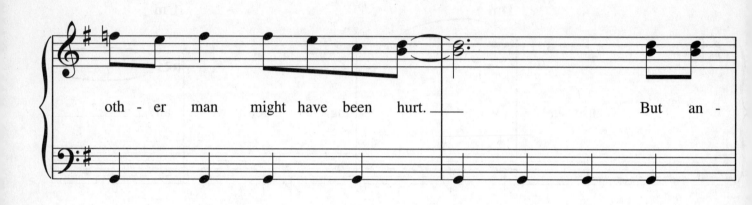

oth - er man might have been hurt. ___ But an -

oth-er man nev-er would have let her go. I stuffed the bill in my shirt. ___

And she walked a - way in si -

G   F   C   G

- lence, ___ it's strange how you nev - er know. ___ But

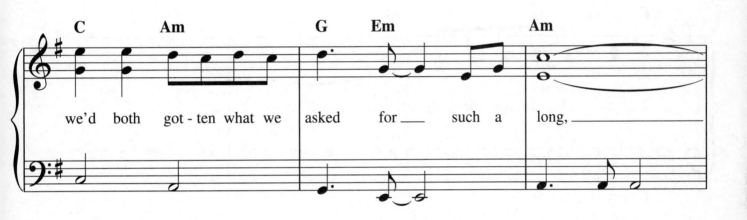

C   Am   G   Em   Am

we'd both got - ten what we asked for ___ such a long, ___

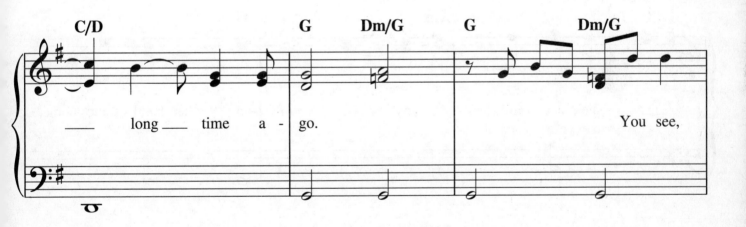

C/D   G   Dm/G   G   Dm/G

___ long ___ time a - go.   You see,

G

she was gon - na be an ac - tress ___ and I was gon - na learn to fly. ___

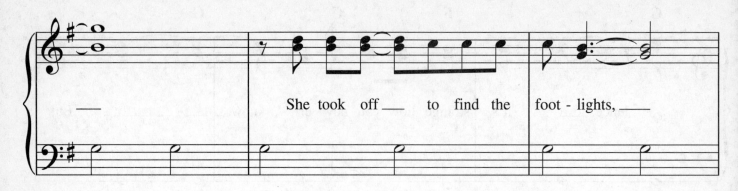

She took off ___ to find the foot-lights, ___

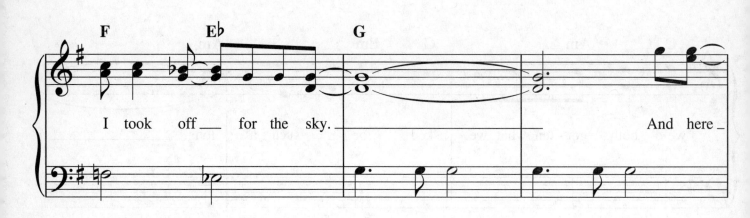

I took off ___ for the sky. ___ And here ___

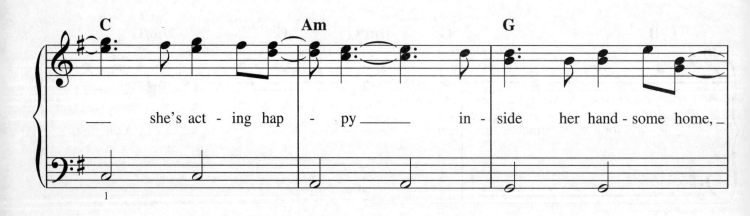

___ she's act-ing hap - py ___ in - side her hand-some home, ___

____ and me, I'm fly-ing in my tax - i, tak-ing

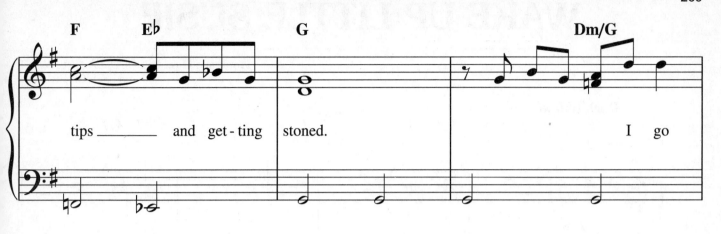

tips _____ and get-ting stoned.   I go

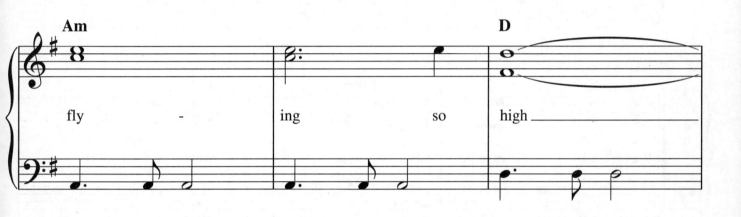

fly - ing so high _____

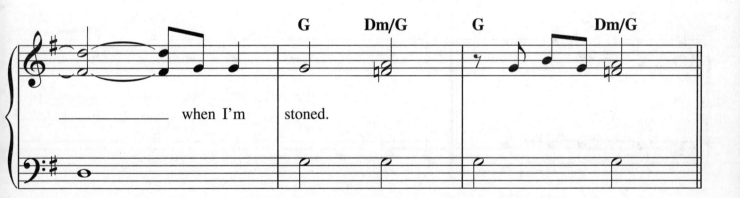

_____ when I'm stoned.

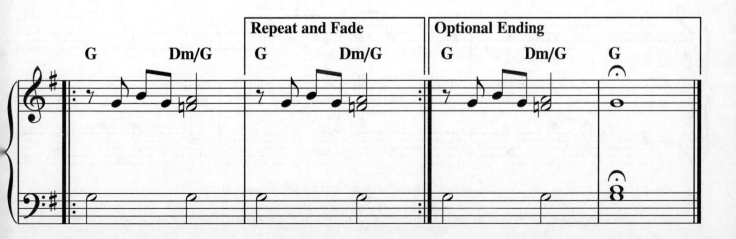

Repeat and Fade

Optional Ending

WAKE UP LITTLE SUSIE

Words and Music by BOUDLEAUX BRYANT
and FELICE BRYANT

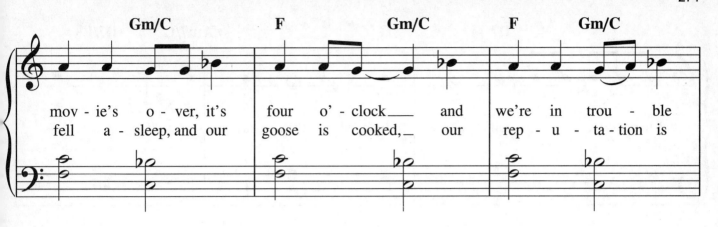

Gm/C   F   Gm/C   F   Gm/C

mov - ie's   o - ver, it's   four   o' - clock____   and   we're   in   trou - ble

fell   a - sleep, and our   goose   is   cooked,___   our   rep - u - ta - tion is

F   G7   F

deep.   } Wake up,___   lit - tle   Su - sie,___   wake up,___   lit - tle

shot.   }

G7   F7   G   D7

Su - sie.___   Well,   what are we gon - na tell   your

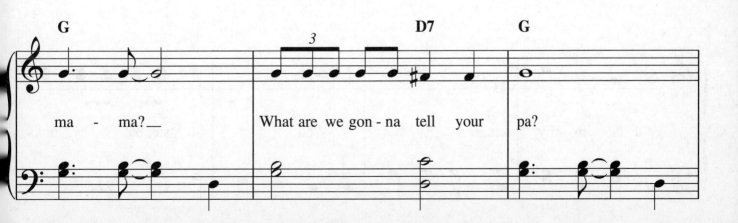

G   D7   G

ma - ma?___   What are we gon - na tell   your   pa?

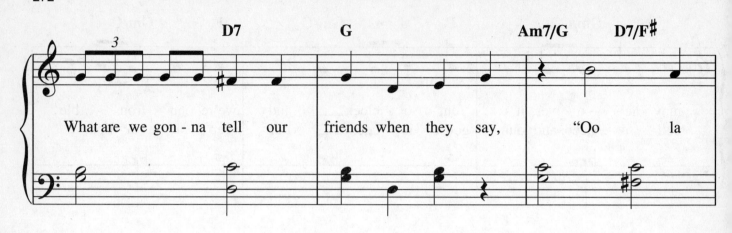

What are we gon-na tell our friends when they say, "Oo la

la?" Wake up,___ lit-tle Su - sie,___ wake up,___ lit-tle

Su - sie.___ Well, we told your ma-ma that

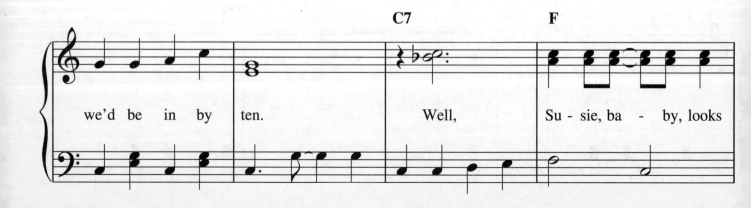

we'd be in by ten. Well, Su-sie, ba - by, looks

WHO WILL SAVE YOUR SOUL

Lyrics and Music by
JEWEL KILCHER

1. Peo-ple liv-in' their lives for you __ on T - V. __ They say they're
bet-ter than you __ and you a-gree. __ He says, "Hold __ my calls" from
be-hind those cold __ brick walls. Says, "Come here, boy, __ there ain't noth-in' for free." __

Additional Lyrics

3. Some are walking, some are talking,
   Some are stalking their kill.
   Got Social Security but it doesn't pay your bills.
   There are addictions to feed
   And there are mouths to pay,
   So you bargain with the devil,
   But you're okay for today.
   Say that you love them,
   Take their money and run.
   Say, it's been swell, sweetheart,
   But it was just one of those things,
   Those flings, those strings you've got to cut.
   So get out on the streets, girls,
   And bust your butts.

WHO'LL STOP THE RAIN

Words and Music by
JOHN FOGERTY

Long as I___ re-mem-ber, the rain___ been com-in' down,___
I went down___ Vir-gin-ia, seek-ing shel-ter from the storm.___
Heard the sing-ers play-ing; how___ we cheered for more.___

___ clouds of mys-t'ry pour-in' con-
___ Caught up in___ the fa-ble, I
___ The crowd had rushed___ to-geth-er,

WISH YOU WERE HERE

Words and Music by ROGER WATERS
and DAVID GILMOUR

So, ___ so you think you can

tell ___ heav - en from hell, ___

lead role ___ in a cage? _____

How I wish, _____

Wish you — were — here. —

THE WORLD I KNOW

Words and Music by ED ROLAND
and ROSS BRIAN CHILDRESS

Oh, it's the world I know.

rit.

WONDERWALL

Words and Music by
NOEL GALLAGHER

G   **Dm7**   **Am**   **C**

feels the way I do a-bout you now._____

Gsus   **Dm**   **F**   **G**

{ And all____ the roads_ we have_ to walk_ are wind-

{ And all____ the roads_ that lead_ you there_ were wind-

Am   **F**   **G**

- ing,   and all____ the lights_ that lead_ us there_ are blind-

- ing,   and all____ the lights_ that light_ the way_ are blind-

Am   **F**   **G**

- ing.}

- ing.}   There are man - y things_ that I____ would

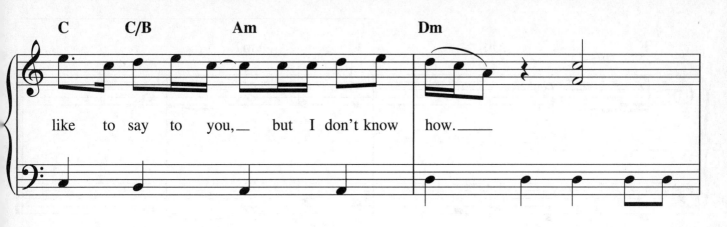

like to say to you,— but I don't know how.——

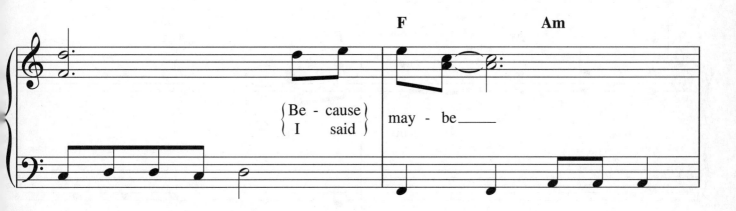

{Be - cause / I said} may - be——

you're gon - na be the one that saves me,——

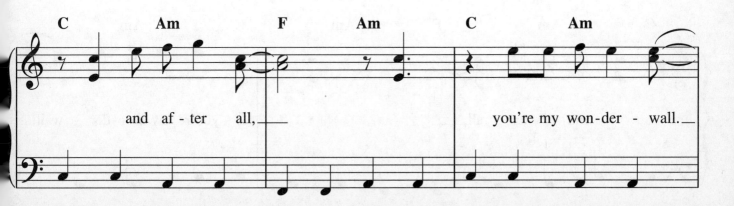

and af - ter all,—— you're my won-der - wall.——

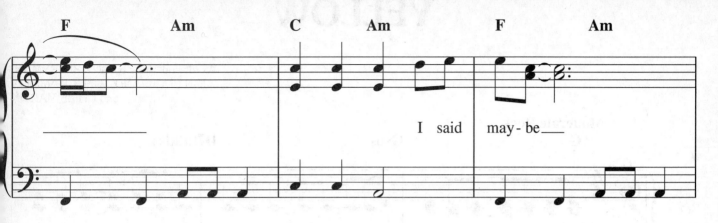

YELLOW

Words and Music by GUY BERRYMAN,
JON BUCKLAND, WILL CHAMPION
and CHRIS MARTIN

301